Interactive Music Therapy –
A Positive Approach

companion volume

Interactive Music Therapy in Child and Family Psychiatry
Amelia Oldfield
Foreword by Dr Joanne Holmes
ISBN 1 84310 444 X

of related interest

Pied Piper
Musical Activities to Develop Basic Skills
John Bean and Amelia Oldfield
ISBN 1 85302 994 7

Filling a Need While Making Some Noise
A Music Therapist's Guide to Pediatrics
Kathy Irvine Lorenzato
Foreword by Kay Roskam
ISBN 1 84310 819 4

Multimodal Psychiatric Music Therapy for Adults,
Adolescents, and Children
A Clinical Manual
Third Edition
Michael D. Cassity and Julia E. Cassity
ISBN 1 84310 831 3

Music Therapy – Intimate Notes
Mercédès Pavlicevic
ISBN 1 85302 692 1

Improvisation
Methods and Techniques for Music Therapy Clinicians,
Educators, and Students
Tony Wigram
Foreword by Professor Kenneth Bruscia
ISBN 1 84310 048 7

Songwriting
Methods, Techniques and Clinical Applications for Music Therapy
Clinicians, Educators and Students
Edited by Felicity Baker and Tony Wigram
Foreword by Even Ruud
ISBN 1 84310 356 7

Interactive Music Therapy – A Positive Approach

Music Therapy at a Child Development Centre

Amelia Oldfield

Jessica Kingsley Publishers
London and Philadelphia

First published in 2006
by Jessica Kingsley Publishers
116 Pentonville Road
London N1 9JB, UK
and
400 Market Street, Suite 400
Philadelphia, PA 19106, USA

www.jkp.com

Library of Congress Cataloging in Publication Data

Oldfield, Amelia.

Interactive music therapy : a positive approach : music therapy at a child development centre / Amelia Oldfield ; foreword by Fatima Janjua.-- 1st American pbk. ed.

p. cm.

Includes bibliographical references and index.

ISBN-13: 978-1-84310-309-7 (pbk. : alk. paper)

ISBN-10: 1-84310-309-5 (pbk. : alk. paper) 1. Music therapy for children. 2. Autism in children. I. Title.

ML3920.O38 2006

616.89'16540083--dc22

2006007242

British Library Cataloguing in Publication Data

A CIP catalogue record for this book is available from the British Library

ISBN-13: 978 1 84310 309 7
ISBN-10: 1 84310 309 5

Printed and bound in Great Britain by
Athenaeum Press, Gateshead, Tyne and Wear

Contents

FOREWORD   9

ACKNOWLEDGEMENTS   13

INTRODUCTION   15

Chapter 1   **Characteristics of my Music Therapy Approach   21**

Orientation   21

How I feel about my work   28

Organisation of the sessions   29

Getting to know the child's musical likes and dislikes   30

My approach to improvisation and music making   32

Single line instruments   33

What I need to survive as a music therapist   35

Parallels between music therapy improvisation and chamber
music playing   36

The unique role of the music therapist in the multi-disciplinary
team   37

Who should be referred to music therapy?   38

Ending the treatment   39

Conclusion   39

Chapter 2   **Working with Pre-school Children with Autistic
Spectrum Disorder and their Parents: Setting
and Case Studies   41**

The Child Development Centre (CDC)   42

Music therapy at the centre   42

Five short case studies   45

Conclusion   61

Chapter 3   **Working with Pre-school Children with Autistic
Spectrum Disorder and their Parents: Characteristics
of my Approach**   **63**
Layout of the room   63
Beginnings and endings of sessions   64
Motivation   65
Structure   66
Balance between following and initiating   68
Basic exchanges   68
Control   72
Movement   73
Playfulness and drama   75
Involving parents or primary carers   76
How my approach fits in with general approaches to autism   80
How my approach fits in with other music therapists' work   83
Conclusion   90

Chapter 4   **Music Therapy with Individual Children
with Severe Physical and Mental Difficulties**   **93**
Three case studies   94
Reflections on these cases   106
Conclusion   114

Chapter 5   **Music Therapy with Individual Children with
No Clear Diagnosis**   **117**
Three case studies   118
Reflections on these cases   125
Conclusion   127

Chapter 6   **Music Therapy Groups at the Child Development
Centre**   **129**
Practicalities   130
Group objectives   131
Group membership   132
Group rules   133
Planning and reviewing   134
What musical material to use in group sessions   135
Four different types of group   135
Conclusion   155

Chapter 7   **Investigation into Music Therapy for Ten Pre-School Children with Autistic Spectrum Disorder and their Parters** **157**

Introduction   157

Literature review   159

Main research hypotheses   162

Methodology   162

Setting the aims   164

Videotaping the sessions   165

Video analysis   165

Interpreting the video analysis data   170

Structured interviews   171

Parenting Stress Index (PSI) forms   172

Results of the study   172

Review of main findings and conclusions   185

Conclusion **189**

Coda   192

APPENDIX 1 'HELLO' SONG   195

APPENDIX 2 MUSIC THERAPY ASSESSMENT FORM (STAGE 1)   196

APPENDIX 3 ON-GOING MUSIC THERAPY ASSESSMENT
FORM (STAGE 2)   197

APPENDIX 4 MUSIC THERAPY REPORT FORM (STAGE 3)   198

APPENDIX 5 DANNY'S MUSIC THERAPY REPORT   199

APPENDIX 6 LEON'S MUSIC THERAPY REPORT   202

APPENDIX 7 GUIDING NOTES FOR PARENTS WRITING ABOUT
MUSIC THERAPY SESSIONS   205

APPENDIX 8 TWO MAKATON SONGS   206

APPENDIX 9 THREE ACTION SONGS   208

APPENDIX 10 EXCERPT FROM A COMPLETED VIDEO ANALYSIS FORM 210

REFERENCES   212

SUBJECT INDEX   217

AUTHOR INDEX   222

List of Tables

Table 1.1   Examples of children's musical characteristics   30

Table 1.2   Comparison between the music therapist and the chamber musician   37

Table 7.1   Video analysis codes for the ten children   166

Table 7.2   Statistical significance of behaviour changes   176

Table 7.3   PSI results for the ten parents   186

List of Figures

Figure 7.1   W's and B's levels of engagement and amount of playing   178

Figure 7.2   H's longest bouts of playing   178

Figure 7.3   E's and B's echolalic speech and spontaneous speech   179

Figure 7.4   I's use of words   180

Figure 7.5   I's, R's and M's negative behaviours   181

Figure 7.6   Mean percentages of Amelia's activities in music therapy sessions across the ten children   183

Figure 7.7   A's percentages of other instrument playing and piano playing across the ten children   184

Figure 7.8   A's percentages of clarinet playing and playful movement across the ten children   184

Foreword

Five years ago I had very little idea of what music therapy actually meant. For most of my professional life I had worked with children with special needs in child development centres up and down the country, and I had never met a music therapist.

There were, of course, references to music therapy in the medical literature, usually as part of a long list of therapies used in this or that particular approach to a specific disability, but I had never stopped to think about what it involved or what it was supposed to achieve.

All this changed when I started to work at the Child Development Centre in Cambridge.

I remember arriving at the Centre one day, for a lunchtime academic meeting, and being surprised by music and sounds coming from behind one of the closed doors around the waiting area. Paying more attention I heard musical noises, as if someone was tuning different instruments. These were intermingled with singing, laughing and fragments of lovely clarinet or piano melodies. My perplexed questioning was greeted with a matter of fact reply from the ladies in reception: 'Oh, it's just music therapy!'

My intense curiosity about what was actually happening behind the door, in that magical world of music and sound, was soon to be satisfied when I met Amelia, who often joined the rest of the team for the lunchtime meeting. Over a period of time, and with her usual, indefatigable enthusiasm, she introduced me to this new and exciting field. She was always ready to tell me about her work, answer all my questions and also provide me with videos and reading references.

As time went on my understanding of the importance and benefits of music therapy became more apparent. This happened through joint practice since many of the children I was following in the clinics were also having music therapy, but also from the positive feedback and enthusiastic comments from parents.

In a child development centre, arriving at a diagnosis and disclosing it to parents can often be a difficult and critical time. Many children referred to us have complex disabilities and a large proportion have autism and autistic spectrum disorders.

No matter how kind and gentle the clinician may be it is impossible to avoid the pain and disappointment felt by parents and the grief which will certainly follow. While the child's difficulties have to be explained in a simple and honest manner, it is important to be able to offer some sort of immediate relief. This could be in the form of a well-structured management plan including emotional and therapeutic support. 'These are Jo's difficulties, we know how hard it feels just now… But, here is what we can do to help him. If we work together things will look very different in a year's time.'

One of the difficulties is that a lot of the therapies and management programmes on offer, no matter how necessary and useful, are often very hard work. This is frequently the case with children with autistic spectrum disorders. Poor co-operation and difficulties in engaging with the therapist are factors inherent in their condition and may lead to numerous attempts at assessment or treatment, which are often quite stressful and negative for children and parents.

In my experience, music therapy is one form of treatment that more rapidly achieves some sort of positive response and engagement from the child. In the early stages of intervention when parents are still burdened with disappointment and fear about their child's future, music therapy sessions may provide the first encouraging and positive experiences for parents. These are not only enjoyable, but allow them to feel more positive and hopeful about their child's progress.

In this book, Amelia clearly demonstrates the power of music not only in drawing the attention and interest of even the most withdrawn children, but also in promoting awareness of the other and lay down some basic rules of interaction. When dealing with severe social communication problems, this breakthrough is essential and should be happening as early as possible in the intervention process. The effectiveness of music therapy in encouraging communication, and the fact that this happens mostly within a relaxed and enjoyable context where there is no apparent testing of the child's abilities, makes it particularly suited to become one of the first services to be involved immediately after diagnosis.

Within a multi-disciplinary team, these initial gains in music therapy could be built upon and extended by other therapists and support workers.

There is, however, one other aspect of Amelia's research that I found par-ticularly crucial and exciting. It was not really a surprise since I had been well aware of how much parents enjoyed their music therapy sessions, but I had not grasped its full potential. I am referring to the possibility of involving parents in the therapy session, showing them how to interact with their child, boost their confidence and, above all, allow them to enjoy the child and feel they can and should be active participants in his or her management. Everyone agrees that, irrespective of disability, parents' acceptance and engagement with their child is essential and one of the most powerful factors determining prognosis. I have no doubts that among all therapies music therapy is best placed to initiate the process of encouraging parents and to achieve their co-operation from the very beginning. This would certainly have positive repercussions on the work of other therapists.

I would hope that more and more clinicians working in multi-disciplin-ary teams will come to know and understand music therapy and recognise its benefits for children with different disabilities. This can only happen if music therapists themselves are prepared to speak up and actively spread their message. Through her clinical and research work, and presently with this new book, Amelia is doing just that, with great benefit for children, families and professionals everywhere.

Dr Fatima Janjua MD MSc FRCPCH PhD
Consultant Community Paediatrician

Acknowledgements

Thank you to all the children and their families I have worked with for providing me with the inspiration to write this book.

Thank you to the parents who have taken the time and trouble to write about their own experiences in music therapy sessions. I have been very moved by what has been said and written.

Thank you to all the people who have allowed me to include photographs.

Thank you to all my colleagues who have helped, inspired and supported me over many years.

Thank you to Fatima Janjua for writing such a warm and sensitive prologue. I was very moved.

Thank you to Maggie Boon and Sue Parlby for allowing me to include their case studies.

Thank you to Malcolm Adams for help with my research.

Thank you to Claire Rawson for writing out the songs.

Thank you to Joy Nudds and Melanie Piper for producing the photographs from the training videos.

Thank you to my husband, David, and my children Daniel, Paul, Laura and Claire, for letting me get on with my writing and being patient and encouraging.

Introduction

It is Thursday morning at the Child Development Centre, Addenbrooke's Hospital, Cambridge. I am expecting to see six pre-school children with their mothers, for about 40 minutes each. Three of the children are on the autistic spectrum, one has had severe behaviour problems and two are multiply and severely physically disabled as well as having severe learning difficulties.

Three-year-old Benjamin, who has recently been diagnosed with autism, walks in with a broad smile and sits on his mother's lap while I sing the 'Hello' song (see Appendix 1). He is quite rough with the guitar when I offer it to him to tap or strum but makes some vocal sounds which he repeats excitedly when I enter into a vocal dialogue with him. When we put the guitar away he screams 'all finished' in recognition of what we are doing. He then dashes to sit in a box trolley at one end of the room, one of his favourite spots. I leave him to his own devices and he sets up a sequence of actions he had started the previous week: lie down in trolley, get up, jump out of the trolley, run to the door, peep out of a crack into the waiting room, turn around and then run back to the trolley. After a minute or two I go over to the trolley, jump with him as he gets out of the trolley, then run with him to the door, making the most of my stamping on the floor by singing an accompaniment to the steps. Benjamin's attention is caught, he looks up at me, grins and a stamping/dancing/vocalising dialogue begins. When his attention wavers he goes back to his trolley/door/peeping routine – but every time he jumps out of the trolley I can capture his attention by jumping and stamping with him. Later in the session, I pick up my clarinet and offer Benjamin a reed horn and our stamping dialogue soon turns into a clarinet and horn dialogue. When the session ends, his mother is delighted to have seen Benjamin being so communicative. I feel elated and excited by our moments of playful interaction.

At the end of the morning, Sean's mother wheels her four-year-old son into the music therapy room. I have been working with Sean and his mother for four months, but we have had many interruptions because of Sean's poor health. Sean is profoundly learning disabled and severely physically handicapped. He has no speech, and is partially sighted. Sean can use both his arms and hands, but his movements are often uncontrolled. I have learnt that Sean takes lots of time to adjust to a new instrument so I spend a long time singing 'Hello' to him and then position the guitar so that he can tap the wood and strum the strings. I improvise a vocal folk song to fit in with his random taps and strums with long pauses in between the phrases. Gradually he seems to be able to control his movements a little and his responses appear to fit into the musical phrases. His mother looks at me, smiles and shakes her head in disbelief. Later, I position Sean's wheelchair at the upper end of the piano and play on the lower end myself. Again I improvise, providing clear shapes to my phrases, but leaving lots of gaps. Sean's mother gently guides his hands to the piano until he gets used to the feel and the position of the keyboard. At first his playing seems random, but very slowly, over a period of about 15 minutes, his playing becomes more definite and frequent and I feel we are having a musical exchange. On two occasions Sean smiles and I am intensely moved by his involvement in the playing. When we have to bring the piece to an end Sean looks desperately sad and is on the verge of tears. I wish I could go on playing with him for much longer. Sean's mother is also very moved by the session and we discuss the idea of videoing it. She says that she would like to show a video of Sean's playing to his nursery teacher as she does not think anyone will believe he can be so engaged.

I have been working as a music therapist for 25 years and sessions such as these two have been occurring and continue to occur every week. This work is tremendously rewarding. It is a privilege to have a job where I can communicate in some way with children and families who usually find this process very difficult. In this book I will write about my work so that I can share my enthusiasm with others and, it is hoped, encourage and enable other music therapists to work in similar ways.

The other reason I am writing this book is because I think that my work has evolved into a specific approach. This approach has some aspects in common with other music therapy approaches but is sufficiently different from other music therapy methods defined in the literature to warrant description.

In this book I will describe my work at a child development centre, working mostly with pre-school children and their parents. I initially became aware that I had developed what seemed to be a specific music therapy approach in my work with children with autistic spectrum disorder, so I will describe this first. I will then go on to describe work with severely physically and mentally disabled children and then with children with no clear diagnosis. I will explore my work in child and family psychiatry in my companion book *Interactive Music Therapy in Child and Family Psychiatry* (Oldfield 2006). Other music therapists work in many different clinical areas such as adult psychiatry, adults with learning difficulties, work with the elderly, with stroke or accident victims, or in prison and probation services.

I have called my particular way of working 'Interactive music therapy: a positive approach'. It is interactive because the (mostly) non-verbal musical exchanges form the basis of the therapy. It is also interactive because I have an active role rather than a passive role, even when I am listening and responding to what a child might do rather than initiating ideas myself.

Like all music therapists I am constantly having to answer the question: 'What is music therapy?' Over the years I have elaborated various answers. I have a 30-second response when asked the question by a neurologist in the lift during a medical conference. I have a 20-minute answer when quizzed by a London taxi driver, or I can provide an explanation through a two-hour in-service workshop session, which includes encouraging members of the multi-disciplinary team to experiment with various percussion instruments. In all these answers I emphasise that I use live and mostly improvised music to enable an interaction to occur. One could argue that all music therapists use interactions in some way or another in their work. However, in my work, the non-verbal improvised interactions are the main focus of the therapy, the core, the defining factor.

I call my way of working positive because I am focusing mostly on the enjoyable, playful and motivating force of music making. This does not mean that a child or a family will not be allowed to express anger or sadness, for example, in my sessions. In these cases the positive aspect of being able to express feelings and give vent to feelings of anger through music making may be emphasised. However, although the feelings and moods of children and families will always be heard and respected, the focus on the enjoyable, playful side of music making is usually at the centre of my work.

I might also help a parent or a child to focus on positive moments in a session in order to build up confidence and self-esteem and then reflect on more difficult or painful moments in a constructive way. The unpleasant moments will not be pushed away or ignored but put into context, enabling families to gain strength to face up to difficulties through acknowledging positive aspects they may not previously have been aware existed.

When I started working as a music therapist 25 years ago I did not start out with a specific approach or idea. Interactive music therapy gradually evolved as I gained experience in three different clinical areas: learning disabilities (all ages), child development, and child and family psychiatry. The process of communicating non-verbally through improvised music making always fascinated me and I often discussed this complex and unpredictable process with other music therapy colleagues or members of the multi-disciplinary teams I was involved with.

During the 1990s I had four children of my own while I continued to work part-time as a music therapist. I learnt a huge amount from being a mother and particularly from communicating non-verbally with my babies. The parallels between the babbling exchanges with my babies and the musical interactions in my music therapy sessions suddenly became much clearer.

The fascination with the processes involved in my music therapy practice has led me to set up four research investigations in various clinical fields and settings with both individual clients and groups of clients. In all four research projects, the results were positive and indicated that music therapy was effective.

Even more important for me was that these investigations helped to define my particular music therapy approach in a variety of clinical areas and confirmed that this way of working was effective and successful. Extensive studies of the literature as well as many meetings and discussions with colleagues indicated to me that, although aspects of my work overlapped with the work of other music therapists, the approach as a whole was characteristic of my work and not generally used by other music therapists.

Since 1994, when the music therapist Helen Odell-Miller and I established a music therapy training course at Anglia Polytechnic University, I have been teaching music therapy students. As these students have qualified I have been involved in supervising some of their clinical work, sometimes over periods of up to eight years. Many of these students have successfully used the specific music therapy approaches that I have developed with particular client groups. Others have adapted my approaches to fit in with slightly different clinical settings or client groups.

Thus, my clinical work, my research investigations and my experience in training music therapists indicate that I am successfully using some specific music therapy techniques and methods that have not been described before in detail. Over the past 12 years I have also produced six training videos that illustrate my clinical work in a variety of settings. Selecting video excerpts for these films and writing the scripts has been another way to help me to clarify and define my specific approach. Although I have previously written several articles about aspects of my work, this book and *Interactive Music Therapy in Child and Family Psychiatry* will describe all these interventions and give many supporting clinical examples. I will describe my music therapy approach, both in general and with specific client groups. I hope these books will be of use both to music therapists and anyone with an interest in music therapy.

Chapter 1

Characteristics of my Music Therapy Approach

In this chapter I describe my general music therapy approach. I look at how this approach fits in with the work of other music therapists, how the approach has evolved and how I feel about my work. Subsequent chapters describe in more detail what characterises my approach with specific clinical client groups such as pre-school children with autistic spectrum disorder and their parents, or children with severe physical and mental difficulties.

Orientation

How my work fits in with other music therapy or psychological models

Wigram, Nygaard Pederson and Ole Bonde (2002) describe five music therapy models: guided imagery and music – the Bonny model; analytically orientated music therapy – the Priestly model; creative music therapy – the

Nordoff–Robbins model; free improvisation therapy – the Alvin model; and finally, behavioural music therapy.

As I trained with Juliette Alvin in 1979, it is not surprising that many aspects of my approach fit into this model. Wigram *et al.* (p.131) indicate that Alvin's method is musical:

- All the client's therapeutic work centres around listening to or making music.

- Every conceivable kind of musical activity can be used.

- Improvisation is used in a totally free way, using sounds or music that are not composed or written down beforehand.

- By sounding the instruments in different ways, or by using unorganised vocal sounds, inventing musical themes allows great freedom.

- Free improvisation requires no musical ability or training and is not evaluated according to musical criteria.

- The therapist imposes no musical rules, restrictions, directions or guidelines when improvising, unless requested by the client. The client is free to establish, or not establish, a pulse, metre, rhythmic pattern, scale, tonal centre, melodic theme or harmonic frame.

Nevertheless, there are aspects of my approach that do not fit in with Alvin's method. Although, like Alvin, my method is musical, I am also clear that I use music as a means to achieve non-musical aims. For example, if I am trying to attract the attention of a child with autistic spectrum disorder who is wandering around the room apparently unaware of anyone else in the room, I might follow the child and accompany his or her movements with improvised music on the clarinet. If the child then looks up at me I might turn away and try to entice the child to follow me. The *aim* is to establish some basic interaction between us. The *tool* I have used is the music on the clarinet, which motivates the child to take an interest in me.

More specifically than Alvin, in my approach I think that it is important, particularly at the beginning of the work, that the children view our sessions as a positive time together, which they want to be part of. As we get to know each other and the child and the primary carer gain my trust, I might, at times, try to encourage the children and their primary carers to do things that they find difficult. If a child wishes to express frustration, anger or sadness, I will provide opportunities for these feelings to be expressed through music making. Nevertheless, the overall experience must remain positive enough for the child to be motivated to come back into the room again the following week. As Coates (2001) indicates, it is essential to develop a trusting and communicating relationship with the child with autistic spectrum disorder. It is my belief that this can be achieved with any clients – but particularly with children – only if the general experience of the music therapy session is a positive one.

For most of the children and families that I work with, the building up of confidence and self-esteem is very important. Families with young children with learning disabilities may have spent long hours talking to specialists about all the things the child cannot do or is doing incorrectly. Often, the music therapy sessions are the first time that a professional is focusing on and enjoying the positive aspects of what the child *can* do. Similarly a mother may have lost confidence in her ability to interact with her child and feel despondent about her capability to be a good mother. By thinking back, with the mother, to improvised musical interactions between the child and the mother after the music therapy sessions, I can point out positive aspects of the mother's interactions with her child which she may be surprised and pleased to reflect on.

Most of the children with whom I work are probably not aware of the therapeutic nature of my intervention. I would imagine that they associate coming to see me with a time when they make music and interact with me through playful musical exchanges. It is usually through the musical interactions that we have that progress occurs rather than through the children gaining insight into their own difficulties.

However, with the parents of the children, I am very clear about what I hope to help with, and we discuss their child's progress at the end of every session. For example, we might agree that it would be helpful to focus on encouraging a child to vocalise, or to remain focused on one activity for longer rather than rushing from one to another. We might also discuss in what way the music therapy sessions are going to help the mothers of the children. For example, some mothers are keen to use music therapy sessions to help their child to be more independent and do things on their own rather than always be on their mother's lap. However, here again there are some aspects that are not always addressed verbally, even though I might have a very clear idea of what I am hoping for. I might, for example, notice that a

mother who is low in confidence is mismatching musically in her interactions with her child. By this I mean that she is perhaps not listening to her
child's musical suggestions well enough, or conversely she may always be
copying her child, never contributing her own ideas, so the conversation
cannot develop. In these cases, I will probably not draw the mother's
attention to this but try to gradually model more effective patterns of interactions, while providing verbal support and encouragement for her. Once
the mother's confidence has grown and she has picked up new ways of interacting non-verbally with her child, it might be possible to help her gain
insight into the learning process that has taken place. As with the child, the
focus is almost always on a positive aspect of the mother's relationship with
her child. As she rejoices in the positive aspects of her interactions with her
child, her confidence will grow and she will feel ready to look at possible
new ways of communicating and playing.

I will be looking at the way I work closely with parents in more detail in
other chapters in this book. I think my close work with parents is a characteristic of my approach and certainly differs from Alvin's approach.

Alvin believed that it was important for music therapists to use their first
instrument in their work and described several case studies where she uses
her cello (Alvin and Warwick 1991). Similarly, I use my clarinet in almost all
my music therapy sessions. As the clarinet is a wind instrument and children
often become quite fascinated by the instrument itself, it could be seen as a
'intermediary object' as described by Winnicott (1972). Wigram *et al.* (2002,
p.132) indicate that Alvin thought that the musical instrument represented a
'safe intermediary object'. However, I think it is the sound the instrument
makes and the fact that I can physically follow the child around the room
that provide the link between the two of us rather than the instrument itself. I
explore these aspects of my work further in Chapter 2. Unlike Alvin's use of
the cello, I do *not* mainly use the clarinet to perform classical music.

Much has been written about the intrinsic power of music to affect the
emotions (Juslin and Sloboda 2001). In my approach, the musical impact on
emotions that are intrinsically social is of particular importance. The fact that
emotions are catching is explained by Juslin and Sloboda (p.86). I would
suggest that this transfer of emotions is enhanced and facilitated by improvised musical interactions.

Bunt and Pavlicevic (2001) indicate that the focus for therapeutic
change lies in the musical relationship built up between the therapist and the
patient. They write:

Patients in music therapy improvise; the music therapist improvises. The participants in any improvisation make personal variations within the musical forms, the process of deciding what to play and how to shape musical events changing from moment to moment. The music therapist values and attends to all the musical communications made by the individual or group member – there is no 'right' or 'wrong' way of playing. In the psychologically and physically safe context of a thera- peutic setting, the different forms of improvisation can also help an individual to try out different aspects of relating both within the self and between people. (p.186)

Certainly the musical relationship I develop with children and families is of paramount importance in my therapeutic work, and the above extract very clearly describes music therapy improvisations in my work. However, my focus is sometimes more on developing interactive patterns, which can then be transmitted to the child and the mother, rather than the main focus for therapy being based primarily on the relationship between the child and myself.

A number of psychological models are relevant to my music therapy approach. Developmental models – such as the example given by Carr (1999, p.25) of Newman's revision of Erikson's psychological stage model – often help to understand what stage a child is at. If a child is putting objects in his mouth continuously, for example, I will accept that this is probably a phase he is going through rather than feeling he constantly needs to be dis- tracted. Nevertheless, some autistic spectrum children do not follow usual developmental patterns and may, for example, use whole sentences before babbling in any way.

Behavioural approaches based on learning theories – such as Carr's guidelines for behaviour-control programmes (Carr 1999, p.131) – are par- ticularly useful when managing aggression or extreme resistance. For instance, I often have to make a conscious effort not to get drawn into negative patterns of behaviours. Some children with autism find that the only way they can interact with adults and feel in control of the situation is by getting that adult to tell them to stop doing something. In these cases, I work hard to react in a very bored way to misdemeanours but give the child lots of excited praise as soon as anything positive occurs.

Psychodynamic theories often help me to understand my work better. Sometimes, for example, I find that I am trying to do too much and not waiting or listening to the child enough. Clinical supervision sessions will help me to realise that I may be picking up feelings of frustration and lack of control from the child by counter-transference rather than these being my own feelings. I am also often aware that the ways in which a parent behaves with her child may be influenced by unresolved issues of grieving for the healthy child wished for, even if on the surface she appears to accept and understand the child's diagnosis. For example, a parent might resent anyone other than herself being able to get through to her child. She wants to be valued as the skilled, good parent who can interact with a difficult child with autistic spectrum disorder in order to compensate for being a 'bad parent' in producing an abnormal child in the first place.

Winnicott's theories (1960, 1972) of 'holding and caring for clients' and being a 'good enough mother' often are relevant to the work I am doing both with children and their parents who also frequently require care and mothering. Even when children struggle to engage in any way, the fact that I am there every week and am trying to help in some way is in itself important for the family.

Daniel Stern's writing (1985, 1995, 1996) on pre-verbal babbling between mothers and infants constantly comes to mind as a parallel to the non-verbal musical interactions I have with the children and the families I work with. In children who are not using speech the musical interactions sometimes lead to vocalisations, then to babbling exchanges and later to the beginnings of speech.

Thus, I do not feel that I subscribe to one psychological model of working, or to one established music therapy model, but am influenced and helped by different aspects of a number of different models. If asked to describe my music therapy approach in one sentence I would say that I have an interactive, positive approach, which involves live and mostly improvised music making.

Life experiences

As I explained in the Introduction, my music therapy approach has evolved gradually from 25 years of clinical work, research and the experience of training music therapists.

The way I work, my approach and the thinking behind my clinical work is influenced also by my personal life experiences. I do not propose to write an autobiography here but would like to mention a few aspects of my past that have greatly influenced my work and made me the music therapist that I am.

Because my father was an international civil servant I have lived in many different countries and grew up speaking three languages. I was born in New York, brought up in Austria, went to a French lycée and attended university and music college in the South of France, Canada and finally the Guildhall School of Music in London. Although I had British nationality and spoke English at home I did not actually live in the UK. Until I came to London to train as a music therapist in 1979, I was always an expatriate; in other words I had a slightly unusual identity. When I arrived in the UK I sounded British, but I certainly did not feel British, and it took me some time to adjust to the fact that I was no longer an interesting foreigner. Gradually I developed a new (perhaps even more exotic) identity as a music therapist. As a result I have been at ease in a slightly unusual profession, have not found it difficult fitting into different multi-disciplinary teams, and have continued to enjoy being slightly special and having to explain who I am and what I do. I have always been intrigued by the identity of the music therapist; how exactly the music therapist's role differs from the rest of the multi-disciplinary team and what special contribution the music therapist makes.

My experience of living in different cultures has made it easy for me to understand families from different social backgrounds and to be open-minded about different approaches to children or family life. The knowledge of languages has enabled me to communicate easily with French- or German-speaking music therapists, to learn not only about different approaches to music therapy but also to be in touch with radically different ways of thinking about the profession. I have always wanted to remain open-minded to different ways of working. This contact with a wide variety of approaches as well as the determination to remain receptive to different ways of thinking about music therapy may have helped me to be clear about my own approach. This approach works for me and is and will be useful to others, but it will only ever be one of many valid music therapy approaches.

I have learnt a huge amount from the experience of having and bringing up four children, including twins. Of course I do not feel that having and raising children is a prerequisite to being an effective music therapist, but I cannot pretend that I have not gained greatly in confidence since I became a mother myself. It is easier to identify with endless sleepless nights, exhaustion at half term and worries about teenagers out late at night when you have experienced these things first hand. Many families also automatically have more trust in a therapist who has had children herself, which can be an advantage. On a practical level, there have been times when coming to work has been more restful than dealing with the family and the house at home. On the other hand it is always wonderful seeing them all at the end of the day and I never have difficulties switching off from work once I get home. In many ways the two occupations have complemented and helped each other. At times my experience of working in child and family psychiatry has helped me to think clearly about and deal with child management issues at home. At work, the experience of having had children enables me to identify more easily with mothers and appreciate how hard and draining family life can be. Since having children of my own it has become even more imperative for me to think of the children I treat in the context of the families and, whenever possible and appropriate, to provide support and help for the parents as well as the children.

How I feel about my work

Working with children with autistic spectrum disorder or severe learning disabilities, for example, can be hard work and frustrating but it can also be very exciting. No two sessions are similar and each child poses new questions and challenges. Nevertheless, I almost always manage to get through to the child or the parent in some way. This motivates me to continue my efforts at communication and the exchanges then can sometimes become extremely rewarding.

Before seeing a child, I will look at the previous week's notes to remind myself of my objectives and important past moments. These moments usually come flooding back to me, reminding me of the quality of our relationship. I always feel a little nervous before starting the session. Even after working in this area for 25 years I wonder whether I will be able to make contact, whether I will find ways of getting through and whether I will recapture past intense exchanges and manage to develop these further. Deep down, I have the confidence to know that contact will almost certainly be established in some way, but perhaps I need this slight tension to give me the adrenalin to sustain my complete focus and attention.

Once the session starts, I am 100 per cent focused on the child and the parent and my anxiety disappears. Parents and observers remark that I must get tired because I am often physically as well as mentally very active. Although I may feel weary before or after sessions, I rarely notice these feelings during the actual work because I am so totally immersed in what I am doing.

In many ways there are a lot of similarities between the way I feel about my music therapy work and the way I feel about performing in chamber music concerts. In both cases I am slightly nervous beforehand, completely involved during the event and usually excited and slightly elated afterwards. I explore other parallels between music therapy and chamber music further on in this chapter. However, the fundamental difference between playing music in a performance and playing music in music therapy sessions is that in the first setting the music is an end in itself whereas in music therapy sessions the music is a means to an end. This is clearly explained by Darnley-Smith and Patey (2003, p.43) when they examine the difference between 'performance improvisation' and 'clinical improvisation'.

Organisation of the sessions

Children and families are referred for music therapy treatment either in writing or verbally by another member of the treatment team. I try to make contact with the family as soon as possible to arrange two half-hour music therapy assessment sessions usually on two consecutive weeks, if possible on the same day, at the same time.

I explain to the family that, in the two assessment sessions, I am aiming to find out whether the parent and I feel music therapy would be a helpful intervention. After each session, I will discuss the work with the family and answer any questions. In most cases, I feel that I will be able to help, and discuss what the family feel should be the focus of my work and formulate some clear objectives. At this point I also discuss the family with the referrer and other members of the team so that we can all agree on appropriate therapeutic objectives. Occasionally, the two-week assessment period is not long enough and I suggest two further assessment sessions. As soon as I have an available space I then set up weekly sessions for the child and the parent. Some children might be referred to a music therapy group if I feel the needs of the child and the parent would be addressed more effectively in a group setting and if there is a space in an appropriate music therapy group. Every six to twelve weeks I review progress with the family and the treatment team and discuss how much longer the work might continue.

Getting to know the child's musical likes and dislikes

In the initial music therapy sessions when I am getting to know the child and the parent, I try to find out where the child and the family are musically. I am interested in whether a child recognises and likes specific tunes or styles, or whether, for example, a child's playing is characterised by repetitive rhythmic units. I find it helpful to think of the four different musical elements, pitch, pulse/rhythm, volume and colour, in order to get as complete as possible a musical picture of the child.

Table 1.1 gives examples of children's musical characteristics. Any of these musical features could apply to the parent(s) of the child as well. In some cases the musical characteristics could be listed in different sections. For example, 'Child reacts to expectant silences' could be seen as a duration and listed under the 'Pulse/rhythm' heading.

Although I am particularly focused on finding out where a child is musically at the beginning of the treatment process, I remain focused on the child's musical characteristics throughout the work and will modify my musical responses accordingly.

Table 1.1 Examples of children's musical characteristics

Musical elements	Musical characteristics
Pitch	• Child always chooses the same note on the piano to play.
	• Child always chooses the same pitch of reed horn, and tries them all until the right one is found.
	• Child often sings two notes in a descending minor third.
	• Child fills in gaps in songs by singing at the correct pitch and following my key changes.
	• Child recognises 'Jingle Bells' and 'Row, Row Your Boat'.
	• Child sings snippets of 'Twinkle, Twinkle'.
	• Child responds to jazzy-type melodies.
	• Child seems to like melodies with wide and unpredictable intervals.
	• Child responds to vocal and instrumental glissandi.

Musical elements	Musical characteristics
Pulse/rhythm	• Child usually uses a consistent steady pulse. Crotchet = 120 (approximately).
	• Child can follow my accelerandi and ritardandi.
	• Child enjoys sudden changes in rhythm.
	• Child enjoys speeding up.
	• Child moves and dances to folk dance rhythms.
	• Child often inserts characteristic rhythmic units into the improvisations (e.g. crotchet, quaver, quaver repeated several times).
	• Child responds to rhythmic versions of his/her name.
	• Child always chooses the same combination of drums to play.
Volume	• Child always plays very loudly.
	• Child loves sudden changes of dynamics.
	• Child responds when I change the volume of my voice.
	• Child enjoys our common improvised crescendi and decrescendi.
	• Child inserts accents into characteristic rhythmic phrases.
	• Child reacts to expectant silences.
Colour/timbre	• Child particularly likes the sound of the clarinet.
	• Child often plays clusters of sounds at the bottom of the piano keyboard and listens intently to the sounds.
	• Child likes all the metal percussion (e.g. glockenspiel, chime bars, wind chimes).
	• Child gravitates towards the wooden percussion (e.g. slit drums, wood-blocks).
	• Child reacts to changes of tone colour.
	• Child enjoys and responds to specific harmonic sequences.

My approach to improvisation and music making

In the music therapy sessions, I play the clarinet and the piano and I sing. I also play the guitar and a wide selection of simple percussion, wind and string instruments. The video analysis in Chapter 7 shows the percentage of time spent on each instrument in the research investigation of pre-school children with autism.

Mostly, I improvise music using the child's musical responses, vocalisations and movements as guidelines. I might, for example, repeat a note or rhythm used by a child and then expand, vary and extend the phrase before waiting for another response from the child. The child's music usually determines my style of improvising. I might base my melodies on snatches of melody previously enjoyed by the child, or I might pick up on the child's quiet or energetic mood. However, as well as being intent on establishing musical dialogues with the child I am also aware of the overall form of the music and will often insert predictable rhythmic or melodic patterns into random atonal exchanges in order to provide a sense of direction for our musical conversations.

At times, I insert well-known tunes into my playing or singing, either to see whether the child reacts to these familiar tunes or in order to regain the child's attention by playing a song I know he or she has reacted to in the past. Sometimes, a child will request a certain tune again and again. At these times I might play the tune in a straightforward way first but then improvise variations of the tune to see how far I can go from the original song before losing the child's interest. If the child's attention wanders I can always come back to the original tune. Even when children do not have an obvious favourite song or tune, I find the theme and variations structure very helpful in my improvisations. Its format provides a reassuring familiar structure I can come back to as well as giving me the freedom to wander musically in whichever way is appropriate at the time.

Although, as I explained earlier, I take my musical cues from the child, I do also try to introduce a variety of styles, rhythms and dynamics into the playing, as I have found that children are often captivated by changes in the music. In addition, children do not always react in predictable ways. For example, the very noisy child may show great sensitivity to a very quiet tune on the recorder, or the very quiet child might be delighted by huge cymbal crashes.

My improvisations aim to pick up and develop the child's musical contributions so that we can have constructive musical dialogues. I try to improvise in styles that will suit each individual child and parent best. Nevertheless, my own musical ideas, preferences and limitations also influence the way in which I play. On the piano, I often find myself playing simple IV–V–I type chord progressions, probably as a result of playing variations of children's nursery rhymes. I also use a lot of modal and folk tunes, using a flattened seventh, in the Dorian mode, for example. This might be because there are a lot of children's folk tunes in the Dorian mode and because I find it easy to improvise in this mode. I frequently play in D minor or C minor, possibly because originally my right hand gravitated towards middle C, and my fingers have become used to the physical shapes of the chords in these keys. I think that another reason why I often play in minor keys is because they are quite near to the modal folk keys and it is easy to switch from minor keys to modal or folk styles. This use of minor keys is not usually intended to create a sad or wistful atmosphere.

On the clarinet, I often play in A minor, which in reality is G minor as the clarinet is a transposing instrument in B flat. This is because the reed horns that I have are pitched at G and C; and as I often offer these reed horns to children and parents while I am playing the clarinet, I have become accustomed to improvising in this key. Quite often, I will be moving around the room while I play, so my phrases might be quite long and flowing with no predictable rhythms to accommodate the child's unpredictable movements. At other times I use quite jazzy styles and rhythms as the clarinet is well suited to this.

In addition, I find that I am influenced by many outside factors in improvisations. If I have been practising a particular piece of chamber music, snippets of phrases will appear in my improvisations. If I have been working on technical aspects such as producing very high notes on the clarinet, I will find that high notes are inserted in unexpected places. If I am moved by a piece of music I hear on the way to work in the car, a tune from that piece might find its way into my improvisations.

Single line instruments

It will be clear from the above that I use my clarinet in most of my music therapy sessions. There are a number of reasons why I think that single line instruments (in my case the clarinet) are invaluable in my work:

- When I am playing the clarinet I can be *mobile*. I can crouch down on the ground and be near a child lying on the floor, or I can follow a child who is moving around the room.

- This mobility also allows me to be *playful* and hide as I am playing, setting up peek-a-boo games or inviting a mother to play with her child.

- Playing the clarinet allows me to have *direct eye contact* with the child, which is more difficult when playing the piano.

- The fact that I can *vary the dynamics and the pitches of individual notes* that I play on the clarinet means that I can change the tone colour of my playing and more easily gain a child's attention.

- The fact that I can *alternate between playing the clarinet and singing* means that children and parents will often be encouraged to vocalise themselves. The fluctuations in tone colour on the clarinet can then lead to the child varying his or her own vocal sounds in response to my playing.

- *The single melody line* on the clarinet automatically means that there will be times when there are silences because I have to breathe and there are no accompanying chords. The fact that less is happening musically can promote listening and attention partly because the single line will be a contrast to continuous harmonic chord progressions on the guitar or piano. The single melody line can also easily incorporate two pitches played by a mother and a child on reed horns or chime bars. The child and the mother will still be able to hear 'where they are' in the playing while at the same time feeling part of a musical ensemble.

- *The physical shape of the instrument* can provide a link between the child and myself, with the child holding on to the bell of the instrument. This is a more direct and intimate link than when the child feels the vibrations of the piano that we might both be playing.

- Playing an orchestral instrument gives the music therapist working in a multi-disciplinary team a very *definite identity* as a musician. Other staff may have played the guitar or have some experience on the keyboard. It is less likely that anyone will play an orchestral instrument, or if they do, that they would be willing to play it at work or use it to improvise with children.

• Perhaps the most important reason for using the clarinet in my sessions is that it is *my principal instrument*, which I love and feel a great affinity for. I am more likely to be able to communicate effectively with this instrument than any other.

What I need to survive as a music therapist

In the UK, music therapy students are required to have their own weekly individual personal therapy during their music therapy training. In addition, all the clinical work they do is closely supervised either at college or on their clinical placement. Although regular weekly or monthly clinical supervision is probably most important for the first few years after qualifying, most music therapists continue to have it throughout their working lives. I have always had at least monthly supervision from experienced clinicians with a variety of backgrounds, such as child psychotherapists, specialist nurses and clinical psychologists. In recent years I have explored a wide range of issues often linking clinical music therapy practice with my experience of teaching students on the Music Therapy MA course at Anglia Ruskin University. I have also often discussed difficult families in supervision where, for example, I have been struggling to support distressed parents, or where I have had to air my feelings of anger or frustration when children or families do not seem to receive enough help or support outside music therapy sessions.

Having regular clinical supervision has meant that if I am concerned or worried about an aspect of my clinical work I can put this worry to one side, knowing that there will be an opportunity to air and discuss the issue in supervision.

In addition to clinical supervision I would suggest that it is just as important for music therapists to maintain and develop their own musical skills as well as to use music for themselves for their own fulfilment and satisfaction. Most music therapists in the UK were amateur or professional musicians before they became music therapists and feel in some way unfulfilled if they do not pursue their own musical interests. I have known music therapists who play in jazz or folk groups in their spare time, who go to salsa dance classes, sing in choirs, conduct orchestras or pursue a passion for Wagner opera. In my case I play the clarinet around three times a week in various local chamber groups or orchestras. I find that if I have not played for one or two weeks I begin to get grumpy and irritable; I really *need* to play for myself. My particular interest in chamber music has led me to reflect on the parallels between being a chamber musician and a music therapist.

Parallels between music therapy improvisation and chamber music playing

At first glance chamber musicians and music therapists may appear to have very little in common. The chamber musician reads music off a part whereas the music therapist plays mostly improvised music. For the chamber musician the aim is to perform a piece of music as well as possible in co-operation with other musicians. Although the music therapist also plays with his or her client, that client is only rarely a trained musician, and the music therapist's aim is to use the music as a way of helping the client in some way rather than performing the music as an end in itself.

However, there are also many similarities between the two occupations. Both the chamber musician and the music therapist rely on musical ability to operate well. The chamber musician must be able to play his part and the music therapist must be able to improvise and play by ear. Both the chamber musician and the music therapist have to listen in thorough and sensitive ways. Both the chamber musician and the music therapist support the people they are playing with. The chamber musician may provide a strong bass line in order to allow the soloist to play the melody line in a particular way. The music therapist may support the client by providing a chord sequence under some erratic percussion playing. The chamber music player may lead fellow musicians both through playing and through body language and gestures. Similarly the music therapist may make musical or non-verbal suggestions to the client and at times choose to lead improvisations.

The chamber musician should always communicate with fellow musicians, and in the same way the music therapist is always adapting to the needs of the client or the parent and carer. For both the chamber musician and the music therapist, the musical interactions are intimate, can be intense and are focused on the people in the room. However, as a contrast to this intimacy, eventually the chamber musician goes public and performs to an audience. Similarly, as a contrast to the intimate interactions between the client and the therapist in individual music therapy sessions, in group situations the music therapist may 'perform' at times and will also always have to negotiate and liaise with other staff.

Because of all these parallels (summarised in Table 1.2) I have often felt that both activities have inspired one another. For example, when working as a music therapist a particular fragment of rhythm played by a child may remind me of a similar corresponding phrase in a clarinet quintet. Similarly my ability to communicate non-verbally with my fellow chamber musicians has been greatly enhanced by music therapy dialogues with my clients.

Table 1.2 Comparison between the music therapist and the chamber musician

Music therapist	Chamber musician
Improvise	Play part
Listen	Listen
Support	Support
Guide/suggest	Suggest/lead
Adapt to needs of client/carer	Communicate with fellow musicians
Negotiate/liaise with other staff	Play to audience

The unique role of the music therapist in the multi-disciplinary team

As a music therapist working in multi-disciplinary teams of therapists including physiotherapists, occupational therapists, speech therapists, clinical psychologists, family therapists, arts therapists and drama therapists, I have often reflected on all our different roles. It would appear that physiotherapists, occupational therapists, language and communication therapists, clinical psychologists and family therapists are called upon when the client needs help or advice regarding a specific problem or area. For example, the physiotherapist might be consulted if a child is walking in an unusual way, or a speech therapist will give advice if a child fails to develop speech. A clinical psychologist might carry out specific tests to evaluate how able a child is intellectually, and a family therapist might explore feelings between family members to try to evaluate the causes and consequences of a child's difficult behaviours.

Music therapists, art therapists and drama therapists, on the other hand, may attempt to help with any of the above difficulties. What they specialise in is the means whereby treatment is provided rather than a specific area of difficulty. This concept may appear obvious but is a fundamental difference, which is often not understood.

As music therapists, our ability to play, perform and improvise to a high standard on several different instruments clearly defines us in multi-disciplinary teams where many other areas of expertise and knowledge are shared and overlap between professionals. I think that the relatively high standard of musicianship required to access music therapy training in the UK has helped establish and define the profession. In other countries where music therapists may not necessarily be proficient musicians and resort to using recorded music or very simple percussion exchanges, the profession has struggled more to become established.

Who should be referred to music therapy?

Music therapists will be asked what types of clients with what types of symptoms should be referred. In some ways everyone could benefit from music therapy, so this is a difficult question to answer. As I explain in further chapters in this book, over the past ten years I have tended to specialise in working with children with communication disorders, often using the music to communicate in non-verbal ways. However, this does not mean that clients with other types of difficulties cannot also greatly benefit from music therapy treatment.

I am often asked whether music therapy is *not* advisable for some clients. In my experience, occasional clients (perhaps one in fifteen) really dislike music therapy, or ask me to talk rather than play and have no interest in music making. Nobody *has* to have music therapy treatment and I try to make it clear that stopping treatment (or not taking up treatment) is always an option. It is often thought that clients who show an interest of some kind in music may benefit from music therapy. I think this is probably true but it does not mean that an interest in music is a prerequisite – many types of clients with a wide range of interests (or very few interests) may benefit from music therapy.

Ending the treatment

In my work with pre-school children, it is often quite easy to plan an ending to my work to correspond with the child starting school. In many of the special schools and primary schools in Cambridge, music therapy is available, so if it is felt that the child would benefit from further music therapy treatment this can often be arranged. However, if no further music therapy treatment is available, I will sometimes go on treating children for longer periods. It can then be difficult to decide if and when to finish, while at the same time considering the needs of children awaiting treatment. I try to prepare the families for endings by giving them at least six weeks' notice and giving positive reasons for finishing the work, rather than focusing on how difficult it is to stop.

Some parents become very dependent on the support they receive from weekly sessions and may be helped by the suggestion of having counselling sessions for themselves. Other families will benefit from a break in treatment rather than stopping altogether.

I will often discuss ending work in my own clinical supervision sessions, as when I become attached to children and very excited about the work I am sometimes the one who is finding it most difficult to finish. I have found that it is rarely the child who is most affected by ending treatment. Children are very used to changes in timetables or personnel at the ends of nursery or school terms and can usually adapt if supported and encouraged by the adults around them. Parents and therapists may find it more difficult.

Conclusion

In this chapter, I have shown that my music therapy work can be described as *an interactive, positive approach, which involves live and mostly improvised music making.* It should also be apparent that a lot of my work involves working closely with parents and that I use my clarinet in almost all my sessions. I hope that it is already clear how very much I enjoy my work and how completely absorbing and fascinating the process of interacting with children through improvised music making can be.

In the next chapters I will describe my music therapy approach in specific clinical situations. I hope that this may be useful to other people working or interacting with these client groups.

Chapter 2

Working with Pre-school Children with Autistic Spectrum Disorder and their Parents

Setting and Case Studies

My work with pre-school children with autistic spectrum disorder and their parents has always fascinated me and is the main reason why I was initially motivated to write this book. It is in this area particularly that I feel I have developed a very specific way of working that I will now describe in detail and refer to later in the book when describing approaches in other clinical areas.

The Child Development Centre (CDC)

The CDC is an outpatient centre attached to Addenbrooke's General Hospital, Cambridge. Children of all ages with a wide range of difficulties will be referred, usually by their GP or by another medical specialist. The majority will first be referred before they are two years old.

Children will be initially assessed and diagnosed by paediatricians who might recommend further medical investigations, or other assessments by the clinical psychologist, the physiotherapists or the occupational therapists. Once a diagnosis is reached the child and/or the family may then be referred to a variety of professionals at the centre for regular weekly group and/or individual treatment.

Staffing at the centre includes specialist doctors, physiotherapists, speech therapists, occupational therapists, a clinical psychologist, a health visitor, a social worker and a music therapist. Staff also liaise closely with other professionals in special schools and voluntary organisations who may not actually work at the centre but may play an important role for the child and/or the family.

Although the treatment approach at the centre is primarily focused on the child who is experiencing difficulties, parents and carers are given as much support as possible and are often closely involved in the treatment.

Music therapy at the centre

History of the music therapy post at the centre

Music therapy was first established at the CDC in 1980. At this time, I was working as a full-time music therapist at the Ida Darwin Hospital, a home for 220 people of all ages with learning disabilities. The consultant psychiatrist who set up the CDC arranged for four hours of my post to be allocated to the CDC. When I left my post at the Ida Darwin Hospital in 1987 to take up a new part-time post in child and family psychiatry, it was decided that I should keep the four hours' work at the CDC, so that the two part-time music therapy jobs could be combined. This has been a very practical arrangement as CDC children who have had emotional difficulties have sometimes been referred to the Croft Unit for Child and Family Psychiatry. Similarly, children attending the Croft have occasionally been referred to the CDC for physical assessments or neurological investigations. It has therefore been helpful working as a music therapist in both places.

Since September 2003, the music therapy provision at the CDC has increased to 12 hours a week and the work is shared between my music therapy colleague and myself.

General description

At the CDC I work in a large treatment room which is used by other therapists when I am not present. The room is well equipped with a piano, a guitar and a wide selection of simple percussion, wind and string instruments. At one end of the room there are some large mobile red screens behind which I store the instruments when they are not in use, but which can be useful for children to hide behind during music therapy sessions, as illustrated in the case study later in this chapter.

Music therapy referrals come from other CDC staff who have already assessed and treated the referred child. My colleague and I receive large numbers of referrals. As our time is limited we both feel that it is best not to be involved in one-off music therapy sessions to assist the team with the diagnostic process, but rather to focus on providing on-going music therapy treatment to children and their families. This is why we do not usually take part in diagnostic assessments at the CDC. Nevertheless, if in the future more music therapy time became available it would be useful to think about the possible role of music therapy diagnostic assessments at the CDC.

At the CDC I treat children with a wide range of difficulties either individually or in groups. However, over the past ten years the majority of referrals have been of children with communication difficulties, many of whom have been on the autistic spectrum.

Increase in referrals of children with autistic spectrum disorder

There has been some debate among staff at the CDC regarding why the centre has recently had so many more autistic spectrum disorder referrals. This could be partly because there is a greater general awareness of the condition and because, as a result, more parents are expressing concerns about children with borderline symptoms. It could also be that the diagnosis of autistic spectrum disorder has broadened and children who previously would have been diagnosed as learning disabled are now being diagnosed as having an autistic spectrum disorder in addition to having a learning disability.

A high proportion of these children are being referred to music therapy because the staff at the centre and parents in the area have become aware that the children can often be helped through regular music therapy sessions. This growing awareness has come about gradually. As I have worked continuously at the CDC for over 25 years and a high proportion of the children I have treated have been on the autistic spectrum, more families are now aware that music therapy can be helpful in this area. The training video I have made about music therapy with children on the autistic spectrum has also now been seen by many parents who will often show the video to other families they know with children with autistic spectrum disorder (Oldfield, Nudds and Macdonald 1999). In general, the profile of music therapy in Cambridge has been raised since the MA music therapy training course started at Anglia Polytechnic University in September 1994. When I started working in the Cambridge area in 1980, this was the only specific music therapy post in the area for children. There are now eight music therapists working with children in Cambridge.

Since the increase in the music therapy provision for children in Cambridge, my work at the CDC has been mainly focused on pre-school children. Once the children reach school age they can be referred on to one of my colleagues working in special schools or mainstream primary schools in Cambridge. This means that I will usually treat children for no more than three or four terms before they start attending school.

Links with families and other professionals

I have always aimed to provide support and help for the families of the children and tried to discuss my work openly with parents after every session. However, in recent years – and in particular since my work with John and Anna described later in this chapter – I have usually worked jointly with primary carers remaining in the room with the child when I have treated pre-school children.

I also make sure I discuss children and families with other staff involved in my cases on a regular basis. Sometimes I request particular help from other colleagues such as physiotherapists who might come to my sessions and give me advice on how best to position a child. On several occasions, I have run groups at the CDC in conjunction with other staff such as speech or occupational therapists (Oldfield and Feuerhahn 1986).

Writing notes and reports

My system of taking notes and writing reports at the CDC is based on the three-stage procedure I described some years ago in an article entitled 'A study of the way music therapists analyse their work' (Oldfield 1993). As I am assessing the child I take some very general notes under these headings: attention/awareness/concentration; ability to accept suggestions or direction; motivation; communication; spontaneity and imagination; and any other comments/suggestions. A blank music therapy assessment form is included as Appendix 2.

After I have completed my music therapy assessment, and if I have recommended that the child would benefit from regular music therapy sessions, I then discuss what my future therapeutic aims might be with the family and the relevant members of the CDC team. These objectives are written into the top of my on-going assessment form, and every week I comment on how I feel I have progressed towards achieving each of the therapeutic goals. Each of the forms can be used for six weeks. As I copy my therapeutic aims on to the next sheet I review progress and if necessary adapt or change my objectives. A blank copy of this music therapy assessment form is included as Appendix 3.

When the treatment is completed, or if I am asked to write a report for a case conference, I bring together all the information contained on the on-going music therapy assessment form. A blank music therapy report form is included as Appendix 4. Examples of Danny and Leon's completed music therapy reports are included as Appendices 5 and 6. Danny and Leon are described as two of the five case studies in the next section of this chapter.

In the music therapy reports I try to be clear about my aims and objectives for the children, which I will have discussed with the parents as treatment progresses. However, I do not always go into details regarding the parents' role in the sessions. Often I will have a hidden agenda which I am clear about in my own mind but I do not feel is necessarily useful to discuss. For example, I might feel that a parent is mismatching by always immediately copying her child's musical interactions. However, the parent may not be strong enough to be criticised in any way but may be able to pick up subtly different ways of interacting musically with the child from watching my ways of interacting.

Five short case studies

I will now present five short case studies of music therapy with pre-school children with autistic spectrum disorder. Although all the children are under five and have a diagnosis of autistic spectrum disorder, I have tried to include very different cases to show the great variety of work in this area. In Joseph's case I have described only his first two music therapy assessment sessions because I wanted to reflect on my work at this initial stage. John and Anna's case describes a longer piece of work with excerpts from an article that I wrote with John's mother Anna. Danny was very withdrawn at first but gradually became able to communicate a little in a non-verbal way. Leon was a little boy whose energetic movements and dancing were central to our work and, in Peter's case, his mother and I had to work through a whole range of resistant and rebellious behaviours. In three of the five cases the mothers actively took part in the sessions. Leon's mother was present but observed quietly rather than taking part herself. In Joseph's assessment, his mother was present in the first session but looked after Joseph's baby brother while I saw Joseph on his own in the second session. As with all the other clients referred to in this book, names have been changed to preserve confidentiality. Some of the following descriptions were included in my PhD thesis (Oldfield 2004) and in a chapter I wrote previously about this work (Oldfield 2001).

Joseph

Joseph was three years old and was referred to music therapy by his home teacher. At the time when I assessed him he did not have a diagnosis, although he clearly had severe communication difficulties and was not talking. A few months later he was diagnosed as having childhood autism. Joseph's mother and 18-month-old brother joined Joseph for his first music therapy assessment session when he took a vague interest in the instruments and in joint music making with me, but found it quite hard to remain focused on any one activity for more than a few seconds at a time. His mother and I both felt that he had been distracted by having his mother and younger brother in the room. We thought that he would not mind coming in without his mother for his second session. I will now describe his second music therapy assessment session where we were on our own together.

Joseph came into the room happily and let me guide him to the chair where we had sung the 'Hello' song the previous week. During the song I had to help him to remain seated but I felt he was distracted rather than reluctant to be there. He turned away from me while I was singing, so when I was encouraging him to play the guitar I made a point of looking away. This seemed to enable him to strum the guitar and allowed us to have our first brief sound exchange. During this exchange he looked up at me several times.

Joseph then got up from his chair and started exploring the room, briefly playing instruments on his way. Whenever I tried to come up to him to play with him, he would quickly move away. At one point he played the piano and I played a responding chord and then quickly moved away, before he had a chance to move away himself. Joseph continued to play and I again responded in a similar way. A dialogue developed. Joseph would look around for me expectantly awaiting my answer. I made a point of making deliberate noisy footsteps on my way back to the piano each time I returned. When these footsteps matched the rhythm of Joseph's piano playing he laughed happily, allowing himself to enter into the game. A minute or two later he allowed me to play the piano with him for a few seconds before moving away.

Later in the session, I encouraged Joseph to sit down again with me having offered him two reed horns to play. I matched his movements and his vocal sounds with my voice and two of my own reed horns, trying to draw him into a dialogue. He then held out one of his reed horns for me to blow while he was holding it. Although I had to encourage him to remain seated once, he managed to remain engaged with me during this reed horn exchange, taking turns, watching and anticipating for several minutes before losing interest.

When Joseph proceeded to wander around the room again I followed him, playing my clarinet and attempting to draw him into a movement and chasing-type exchange. Joseph vocalised and laughed in response to my playing and I alternated between vocalising and playing my clarinet.

Towards the end of the session, Joseph and I were able to have a brief percussion exchange, taking turns on the drum, cymbal and slit drum. Again, I over-emphasised my movements, and made sure I was never too close to Joseph.

Clearly, this was a very interactive session, where I felt that I was able to use my music to communicate with Joseph. I had no hesitation in recommending that Joseph should continue with weekly individual music therapy sessions.

John and Anna

John was diagnosed with autistic spectrum disorder when he was two-and-a-half years old. Shortly after he was diagnosed he was referred to me by the paediatrician at the CDC. His mother, Anna, had noticed that he would calm down when recorded music was played to him and at times seemed to try to join in by moving and vocalising.

In his two initial assessment sessions, I saw John with his mother as he was clearly not happy to separate from her. During these two sessions, John resisted any offers of instruments from me, pushing or throwing away anything offered. If I persisted he quickly became very angry, screaming and crying loudly. However, he did seem to listen to the music I played to him, and was particularly responsive to dynamic or rhythmic changes, or when the music suddenly stopped or started. He was also very physically active, rapidly moving from one thing to another.

In spite of his resistance to my suggestions, I felt he was very responsive and sensitive to music and that it would therefore be worth offering him some regular music therapy sessions. When I consulted his mother about what she felt were the most important areas to work on, she immediately said 'speech and communication' and we also agreed that he needed help with concentration and with accepting adult direction.

In his third session, I did attempt to see him without his mother. But this was a disaster, with John screaming in a very distressed way, and his mother very anxious outside listening to his cries, so I invited her to come back in with him after no more than ten minutes.

During the first four months I established a clear structure to the sessions, with familiar 'Hello' and 'Goodbye' songs which were repeated on the same instruments in the same part of the room every week. In between these two points I consciously alternated between encouraging John to do something with us (such as playing the xylophone on the mat or running around playing large percussion instruments), and allowing him to do whatever he wanted while I accompanied his movements and actions by singing or playing other instruments. I have explored this idea of balancing following and initiating with a number of different clients in a previous article (Oldfield 1995).

I was also particularly careful to pick up on John's many vocal sounds, imitate them, answer them and weave them into the musical improvisations. In addition I would often sing or chant commentaries to go with what John was doing at the time: 'John is playing the drum' or 'John and Mummy are having a cuddle'.

Three weeks after our work began this is what Anna wrote:

> [While] John and I were travelling home in the car after a music therapy session, John started saying 'Muma' repeating the word *Mummy* I had just said to him in the same way that we had been repeating vocal sounds to one another in the music therapy session we had just had. I remember the feeling of sheer joy and total disbelief. My son had said a word, something I thought would never happen. I cried as I repeated the word *Mummy* over and over, the first word he had ever said. I was convinced from that moment that music therapy had given my son the pathway to speech. (Jones and Oldfield 1999, p.168)

Initially, John responded very well to the clear structure of the sessions where I alternated between providing some direction and allowing myself to be led by him. However, after about four months, John became more and more resistant to being directed in any way and would fight and struggle fiercely when his mother tried to hold him on her lap even for one minute. After a couple of very stressful sessions we decided to stop being directive in any way if John started resisting or fighting our suggestions.

Three or four sessions later, John surprised us. He had clearly become used to the on/off approach, and when we stopped providing this structure, he found his own way to have time out and then rejoin us. When he felt he had had enough of interacting with us, he would disappear into a little playhouse behind some screens in a corner of the room. After a few minutes, he would return, quite happy to sit and play with us on the carpet with the instruments for a few minutes before disappearing again. Each time he retreated behind the screen he would say 'bye-bye' and then greet us again excitedly as he reappeared. I would leave silences while John was invisible but respond to any small vocal sounds he made. Gradually John came to anticipate and enjoy these blind vocal exchanges, usually bursting into fits of laughter before re-emerging with loud 'hello's. At home, John repeated these games, hiding behind the furniture and rushing out yelling 'see ya' at the top of his voice.

As sessions progressed, John spent less and less time behind the screen. Occasionally, when we felt that he was beginning to be frustrated or upset, his mother or I would suggest that he might like some time out by saying 'bye-bye' and pointing to the screen. Sometimes this worked well and allowed John to retreat for a minute or two without getting too distressed.

During his last few months of music therapy sessions with me and his mother, John seemed more relaxed, having fully understood the structure of the sessions, and feeling he had some control over the situation. He would often choose instruments for his mother and me to play, and he particularly enjoyed making full use of the dynamic range of the instruments by playing soft music to put us to sleep and loud crashes on the cymbal to wake us up. His games were always incredibly intense and engaging and it was impossible not to be completely engrossed in his interactions.

John made a great deal of progress during his two years of individual music therapy sessions with me and his mother. From saying no words he ended up using three- or four-word sentences. Although he still found it hard to remain engaged in any one activity for very long, his concentration became more focused and intense. He still enjoys being in control, but he can now be guided more easily and will get over 'upsets' much more quickly. Anna obviously thoroughly enjoyed being part of our work together. In our joint article she wrote:

> I remember thinking that it was a good thing that John hadn't wanted to stay in the room without me. It was a delight to be able to see John, who usually took no notice of anyone or anything for any length of time, become totally engrossed in making sounds and music. His enthusiasm and pleasure were so intense that it was impossible not to feel happy myself, especially when he started to share his enjoyment with me, bringing me instruments to look at or rushing up to me to give me an excited hug. (Jones and Oldfield 1999, p.168)

Shortly after John and Anna finished their work with me, John started attending a school for children with special needs. In his second term at this school he took part in a music therapy group with a colleague of mine working at the school. Excerpts from a video of this group, filmed after he had been taking part in this group for a year, are included in the music therapy training video mentioned earlier (Oldfield *et al.* 1999). In this session John is able to listen, take turns and generally conform socially while still enjoying the freedom of improvising and performing. Recently, I have heard that he has made so much progress that he has moved to a mainstream school where he is being supported by a classroom assistant.

For me, working with John and Anna was both fascinating and very rewarding. Writing a joint article with Anna provided me with great insight into how she had perceived our work together and convinced me that I should always aim to include mothers (or primary carers) in my individual music therapy sessions with children with autistic spectrum disorder.

This case has been described in two articles (Jones and Oldfield 1999; Oldfield 2001) and is included in a training video ('Matthew' in Oldfield *et al.* 1999).

I have included this case here because it was one of those that made me begin to realise that there were a number of aspects of this work that were specific to my approach with young children with autism. In particular I realised how important it was to work closely with parents and how the use of the clarinet might encourage a child to vocalise and then to talk.

Danny and Liz

Danny was two-and-a-half years old, with a diagnosis of childhood autism. He was referred to music therapy at the CDC by his health visitor. I saw him and his mother for two half-hour assessment sessions followed by 24 weekly music therapy sessions over a period of seven months, with some interruptions because of school holidays.

It took Danny a few weeks to get used to the room and the structure of the sessions. He liked to wander around the room, briefly exploring the musical instruments on his way. He would look at me and show interest when I made a clear musical change, but it was difficult to sustain a sound dialogue. He would resist being guided or physically encouraged in any way and protested by briefly screaming and crying when his mother or I stopped him climbing on furniture. However, he did not persist in drawing us into conflict, and he gradually became content to be in the room with us, having understood and accepted the structure of the session.

I consciously alternated between actively encouraging Danny to interact in some way with me and allowing him to roam freely while I accompanied his movements or his playing. In his free wanderings Danny sometimes became involved in repetitive activities such as turning wheels, but he did not persist for very long in any of these activities and I did not feel he was particularly trying to isolate himself from us.

Gradually, he became aware of and interested in my imitation of his stamping movements, half smiling at me and accentuating his footsteps.

From the very first assessment session, Danny had shown a definite interest in a game where the bells fell off my head on the word 'down' in the song 'London Bridge is Falling Down'. He would watch me and listen to my singing intently while I sung the song and placed the bells on my head, his head or his mother's head. Later, Danny also became very excited when I made a glissando vocal sound accompanied by a sitting down jump at the piano. At this point he clearly looked at me expectantly three or four times, waiting for my response. He smiled and showed awareness that we were sharing an interest. Later in that same session, Danny vocalised in response to one of my glissando sounds. He repeated a vocal sound three times, appearing to experiment with the type of sound he was making.

Danny's mother, Liz, was quite quiet and self-conscious, but gently encouraged Danny and supported my work. She was pleased by the small signs of progress we were seeing and seemed to enjoy helping him to jump in the session or taking part herself, although she was initially shy about playing the instruments. As sessions progressed she gradually picked up on the way I was interacting with Danny through sounds and would play the reed horn at the times when I used my clarinet to follow his movements around the room. In between wandering with me, Danny would go to find his mother, climb on her lap and wait for her to play the horn to him. She would time her playing very sensitively, waiting until he turned to her expectantly, and was clearly delighted when he was pleased with the sound she had made.

Initially, I would often play alongside Danny, copying his rhythmic phrases and improvising around the sounds he was making. Very gradually, Danny came to expect musical responses from both myself and his mother. As sessions progressed he began to make his intentions clear to both of us, sometimes pointing or guiding his mother's or my hands to whatever he wanted to play.

Danny clearly became more communicative and interactive during his music therapy treatment. Liz gradually became more involved in the sessions herself and enjoyed talking about the sessions with me and feeling part of what seemed to be a positive experience for Danny.

Leon

Leon was three years old, with a diagnosis of childhood autism. He was referred to music therapy at the CDC by the speech therapist. I saw him and his mother for two half-hour assessment sessions followed by 25 weekly music therapy sessions over a period of eight months, with some interruptions due to illnesses or holidays.

From the very beginning Leon developed an interest in a rhythmic exchange where he made clicking sounds by tapping two drum beaters together and would excitedly await my response on two similar beaters.

As sessions progressed our beater/tapping exchanges extended to include movement and dance all over the room, and I started to give the percussion variety and shape by adding sung phrases. Leon watched and anticipated my responses and was able to initiate his own ideas as well as copying my suggestions. He enjoyed my responses to his musical suggestions and looked at me expectantly, awaiting my answers. We also developed very interactive clarinet dances where I moved around the room with Leon and we picked up on each other's movements and rhythms.

Over the months Leon's playing and musical exchanges with me became more complicated and varied. He showed awareness and sensitivity not only to phrase endings but also to changes of tempo and musical style. He would react excitedly when the music became louder and faster, or when there was an expectant silence. He quickly responded to the predictable structure of the sessions and clearly expected the familiar 'Hello' and 'Goodbye' activities.

Although Leon was rarely happy to sit down for more than a few minutes, he became able to accept sitting down for the initial 'Hello' activity and was gradually more tolerant of my suggestions. For example, it took me several months to show him how to blow down the wind instruments to produce a sound. For many weeks I would play the clarinet and hand him a wind instrument which he would rather reluctantly take from me and quickly put down after one or two unsuccessful attempts. However, he let me persuade him to have one or two tries every week. Eventually he produced a sound by accident and very much enjoyed blowing down the recorder from then onwards.

In the last few sessions he had great fun with an activity where his mother and I pretended to be asleep and he would then wake us up with great bursts of delighted laughter. Even when he was reluctant to become involved in playing an instrument that I offered to him he would consent to try it once or twice before firmly putting it back on the shelf with the other instruments.

Leon usually made it very clear to us what he wanted to play and when he wanted to finish whatever he was doing. At times he could remain focused on a particular activity for five minutes, but often he would bring games to a close after one or two minutes. Once he had decided that he had had enough it was very difficult to re-engage him in that particular game.

Over the weeks, Leon vocalised more and more as we played and I have tried to develop these sounds into brief vocal exchanges. His vocalisations were varied and creative and he often sung a perfect descending fourth. However, he also sometimes copied snatches of phrases that I initiated. After a couple of months he would reliably say 'ei-ei' for 'bye-bye' when we played the bongos at the end of the session.

Leon's mother was very supportive throughout the sessions, gently helping Leon in unobtrusive ways. At times, she expressed frustration at Leon's inability to remain focused for very long. But she was delighted by his energy and enthusiasm and by the fact that he vocalised and communicated in more sophisticated ways as sessions progressed.

Overall, I feel that Leon made very good progress in his music therapy sessions. As his vocalisations increased he started using some words. His concentration improved and he became more willing to take up other people's ideas or suggestions. Above all, he showed how very much he can enjoy communicating with us through playful sound exchanges. He had an infectious sense of fun, which he wanted to share with both myself and his mother.

Peter and Karen

I saw Peter and his mother, Karen, for weekly music therapy sessions for a year. Peter was just three when I started seeing him and had been diagnosed with autistic spectrum disorder.

Peter was a very engaging and fascinating little boy who would sometimes be very happy and completely immersed in music making and at other times protest vehemently, screaming and shouting whatever Karen or I suggested or did. He was also very unpredictable and I would never know from one week to the next whether he would be happily engaged or locked in battle. Karen and I worked closely together to try to help him. When our sessions finished, I asked her whether she would like to write down some of her thoughts about Peter and our sessions together. I gave her a sheet with some questions to use as a guideline, which are included as Appendix 7.

KAREN'S ACCOUNT OF PETER'S EARLY YEARS AND DAILY LIFE WITH HIM

Peter was an easy baby and from the moment he was born I already loved him very deeply. He was always contented and never seemed to need anything. This was a relief to me as my daughter, Loren, was only 18 months at the time he was born.

Peter started to become more of a handful as soon as he became mobile. He quickly became an expert climber and seemed oblivious to danger. My initial concerns about him started when he was around 18 months old. He seemed to be more distracted than other children and didn't show any interest in playing with toys or myself. He just wanted to do his own thing, which was often dangerous. I couldn't leave him out of my sight for one minute because I was so worried he would hurt himself.

At this stage he didn't seem to be developing in the same way his sister did. If he was hungry or thirsty, for example, he would just go and help himself from the fridge. Part of me felt proud that he was independent at such an early age. I tried to believe my friends who told me that all children were different, and that Peter was just a very independent and strong-minded child. While some of my friend's children were already talking, Peter wasn't even showing signs of being interested in it. He did say a few words at 15 months, but he didn't build on them and even stopped using these words. At the time, however, I put this down to the fact that we are a bilingual family, and many children in multi-cultural environments talk later.

Because he was such an active child, I tried to focus on his physical strengths by taking him to 'Tumble-tots', a soft play group for pre-school children. He absolutely loved climbing on the equipment but it was extremely hard work for me as he wouldn't listen to instructions, wait for his turn or sit down during song time. He didn't seem to understand when or why I was reprimanding him and when I tried to hold him back this would lead to huge tantrums. However, I persisted in taking him, hoping that he would eventually fit in and admiring the well behaved children around me.

At around 20 months, I decided to try to encourage Peter to become more interested in toys and games by taking him to a 'Fun for 2s' play group where parents and children join in art and craft, pretend play, sand games and songs. Peter again was very interested in everything, but kept wandering from one activity to another, not really settling on any one thing. With lots of effort on my part, he was able to do some of the art and craft; however, he mainly played on his own and would have tantrums if he could not have the toy he wanted.

At this time, I started to seriously doubt my parenting abilities, and would question other mothers to try to find out what the magic touch was that I lacked. I tried putting Peter on an additive-free diet. I even took part in a research project looking at how children start relating to other people and develop friendships.

When Peter had his developmental check, he didn't do any of the activities that were suggested to him. I remembered how eager my daughter had been to participate and achieve. At this point I asked for further investigations. The heath visitor sent me to my GP who in turn referred Peter to a hearing specialist and the CDC.

The hearing test went fine, but at the CDC, after our first meeting, we were warned of the possibility that Peter might be autistic, and a second appointment was set. From that moment I knew something was wrong and, after researching about autism, I knew even before the second meeting that Peter was autistic. It made sense but it wasn't easy. Even now I'm still hoping that everybody got it wrong, that it is just a temporary developmental delay and that he is going to catch up, or wake up one morning and come to me and say: 'Hey Mum, I got you there!'

Facing reality wasn't easy, I was so much hoping for a normal, happy family...

Daily life is quite hard work. I'm always catching myself assessing Peter, looking at what he is doing well and praising him warmly and looking at his difficulties and trying to find a way of helping him and reaching him. Given his difficulties he is a very good boy and is doing extremely well, but to me it's not enough. Even though I know there is no cure, I want to find a way to beat autism and above all to make Peter happy. It really breaks my heart when I see him struggle and get frustrated. I just want him to have a normal life and be happy.

Unfortunately Peter's autism has had repercussions on everybody in the family:

- Peter's father still doesn't really want his family (with the exception of his parents) to know.

- Loren feels that we are very unfair towards her because Peter is allowed to get away with things that she wouldn't. We are more lenient towards him and she can see that. In addition to that, we have had to give up using two languages at home which means that I can't use my mother tongue any more with the family, and Loren has missed out on a second language.

- I have been through a period of depression and still cry when talking about Peter. I have had to give up on my dream of a normal family and feel badly let down by life.

Nevertheless, Peter seems to be a happy child. His giggle is infectious and will often cheer me up. Whatever we do, he is up for it: swimming, camping, going to the fair... He is a very loving child and is always ready for a hug or a cuddle with me, rough play with his father or a run around with Loren. He is very active and is very much part of the family. Peter has started to want to share things with me and will proudly show me a scribble on a piece of paper. He is my son and I love him.

MUSIC THERAPY WITH PETER AND KAREN

Karen was not sure that Peter would benefit from music therapy. She knew he liked music because he would dance around when he heard music and jump up and down to certain advertisements on the television and enjoy it when she took out her guitar to play. She had also noticed that classical music sometimes calmed him down, and that he liked action songs at bedtime. This was why she wanted to give music therapy a try.

Peter was initially excited about being in the music therapy room and wanted to play many of the instruments. He was very aware of the sounds around him and noticed changes in style, volume and colour. He clearly recognised 'Twinkle Twinkle' and 'The Wheels on the Bus'. He was happy to choose instruments to play but would also usually accept my suggestions. He would often choose the horns to blow and would walk around the room playing, enjoying my peek-a-boo games as I followed him, playing the clarinet. At other times he would choose the drum and the cymbal and play very loudly and creatively, improvising freely while I played the piano. He particularly loved being in control musically and was delighted when I responded in the way he wanted me to. Peter would often interact very intensively with me in our musical dialogues and would enjoy exchanging ideas and taking turns. However, it was sometimes difficult to sustain his interest for very long, and his music making could be a little random, without clear direction or structure.

This is what Karen wrote about her first impressions of music therapy with Peter:

> [At first] I wasn't sure what to expect. How could my son improve through music? How could music help him?... At the first session, I felt a bit awkward. Peter was given drumsticks which he received with a massive smile and I was given drumsticks which I received with perplexity... Was I expected to do something? ...but Amelia made it easy for me by saying to just join in if and when I felt like it, it would show Peter what was expected of him. The idea was that I shouldn't be excluded, I should be part of the process in order to help Peter... In

general, I had a very positive first impression because Peter really enjoyed himself. I wasn't too sure how it worked but I did understand that it was to do with listening and communication via music.

During the year Peter went through periods where he had favourite instruments and activities which he would frequently choose. For example, at the beginning he particularly liked the 'London Bridge is Falling Down' song where bells would fall off our heads on the word 'down'. A little later he developed a game where we would hit the red screens in the room with beaters, echoing each other's rhythms on each side of the screen. He also went through a stage where he would collect up beaters and store them in the top of his shirt, carefully placing the round ends near his neck.

Overall, Peter enjoyed music therapy sessions, would always become engaged in some way and would usually spend some time during each session enthusiastically playing and dialoguing with me.

However, Peter would also sometimes protest vehemently when asked to do something or when something was suggested to him. On several occasions he had to be carried into the room and would take some time to decide to try taking part. It was interesting to note that after difficult beginnings to sessions he usually indicated that he wanted to start the 'Hello' song again from the beginning after he had finished protesting. He appeared to want to make a fresh start, as if he wanted the structure of the music therapy session to remain the same even though he had protested. It seemed as if Peter's rebellious behaviour was to do with him wanting to be in control, rather than because there was a particular instrument or activity he did not like. Karen and I tried lots of different strategies to help him through his protests. Sometimes it helped him to have an instrument to play loudly on and for me to accompany him equally loudly. At other times, he could be distracted by being offered something new and unexpected to play. Mostly, we both just had to wait until he was ready. His internal struggle at these times was obvious. He desperately wanted to take part, but did not feel he could give in, having made a point of protesting.

It was very difficult to predict from one week to the next how the music therapy would go for Peter. In many of our sessions Peter appeared relaxed and at ease, making suggestions but also easily accepting my ideas as well as conforming to the general structure of the session. On other occasions, Peter would have difficult beginnings but then appear to decide that all was well and enjoy the rest of the half-hour with me. At times all would be going well and he would suddenly refuse to stop playing an instrument and become angry and cross whether we tried to continue to play the instrument he wanted, or whether we encouraged him to move on.

Karen and I would discuss his difficulties after sessions and we both agreed that it was important for Peter to realise that we would still be there for him even if he protested and misbehaved. He usually wanted to give his mother a hug once he had gone through a tantrum. My way of showing I still cared for him was by continuing to enjoy our music making even after having been rejected and shouted at.

This is what Karen wrote about Peter's behaviour in the music therapy sessions:

> During the music therapy sessions, I was very aware of Peter's response or lack of response to the music making. For some reason, I feel it very strongly when Peter is distressed and it can affect my mood. Consequently, if a session went fine and he wasn't distressed, I would feel very positive. It was great to see him get out of his 'I want, I don't want' vicious circle without too much frustration. On the other hand, I would feel extremely helpless when his tantrums were distressing him and I wasn't able to help him. I would blame myself for not being able to reach him. But I realise that it is only through challenging him that we will be able to help him to understand that it is OK (and beneficial) to follow instructions and to accept help. It is hard to see him getting stuck in a vicious circle of protest but it is necessary to challenge him in order to help him. The music therapy setting and Amelia's support made it easier to bear.

As the year progressed Peter used the instruments and our musical interactive games in more and more sophisticated ways. In our musical improvisations, he gradually used more complex rhythms and explored a wide range of dynamics and styles. He invented lots of different musical games, including one where he strapped bells to the Velcro fastening on his shoes and walked around holding bells in each hand as well as having bells attached to his feet. Another favourite at the end of our work together was pretending to shoot me by pointing the chime bells at me and then waking me up with cymbal crashes while shouting and singing 'wake up'.

In the first six months, Peter would sometimes vocalise in music therapy sessions but it was particularly noticeable that his babbling increased as he played with toys while he and his mother and I reviewed the music therapy session. Perhaps there were too many sounds to focus on during the session to be conducive to babbling. But the musical stimulation of the session may then have enabled Peter to vocalise more to himself in the quieter period after the music session. At the end of our work together Peter was using more words, which he would sometimes whisper, but at other times could say very clearly.

Overall, Karen felt that Peter had definitely benefited from his music therapy sessions. She thought that his listening and turn-taking skills had improved and that he had become better at accepting direction. She was also particularly impressed with how he had made links between music therapy and home and related an incident early on in his treatment:

> Peter would usually ignore visitors to our house, carrying on with whatever he was doing. However, shortly after he had started music therapy sessions we had several family members coming to eat at our home. Peter went to his music box and took out various toy instruments which he then proceeded to hand out until everybody had an instrument. He then ran back out and went to fetch his toy microphone. He started singing and encouraged everyone to play and follow his lead. Everyone joined in happily and we even had a little sing-song. This was quite a remarkable level of communication for Peter who doesn't speak!

Karen also told me that Peter had taken the 'waking up' game home and was often attempting to wake up members of the family, not only during the day but also in the morning when they were all really asleep!

Throughout our work together, Karen was very warm and caring with Peter and he would often seek reassurance and hugs from her. However, she could also be firm, setting clear boundaries and sticking to them when necessary. She was always pleased to discuss his general progress and his rebellious behaviours with me after the sessions, which I think was useful for both of us.

Karen wrote about what *she* enjoyed in the sessions with Peter and why she felt it was important for us to work together:

> I liked to see Peter enjoying himself and learning through music. I liked to see him overcome his frustration and anger. I liked the fact that Amelia always found something positive to say about the session, even if the whole session was spent dealing with his protests. To be selfish, I liked to feel that I was doing something to help him.
>
> Initially the parent can act as a bridge between the child and music therapist, the relationship and trust between the child and the parent enabling some form of connection between the child and the therapist.

The parent is the child's point of reference. By participating in the session, the child is reassured and knows that nothing bad is going to happen. This will allow the child to start to trust the music therapist and allow himself to participate.

Most of the time I would follow Amelia's guidance and try to encourage Peter to participate by participating myself. At other times I would sense that Peter needed a change, or that he wanted to go in a particular direction, and would convey this to Amelia who would then act upon my suggestion and respond appropriately. The success of music therapy somehow depends on the partnership between the therapist and the parent. The parent knows the child. The therapist is a specialist who knows how to use techniques, has seen lots of different children and can draw on her experience. They need each other to provide the best set-up for that particular child: the conjunction of the knowledge of the subject and the knowledge of the child. It needs to be a partnership.

Conclusion

These five different cases have shown how varied the work with pre-school children with autistic spectrum disorder and their parents can be. However, there are also many similarities and, over the years, characteristics of my approach with this client group have emerged. These will be explored in the next chapter.

Chapter 3

Working with Pre-school Children with Autistic Spectrum Disorder and their Parents

Characteristics of my Approach

In this chapter I elaborate on various aspects that I feel are crucial to my work with this client group.

Layout of the room

Music therapy at the Child Development Centre (CDC) takes place in a large room, which is set up in the same way every week. The instruments are laid out on shelves within reach of the children in one part of the room, two big red screens stand in another part of the room, and there is a large red mat for children to lie on in the centre of the room. Two small chairs are placed to one side of the piano for the child and the mother to sit on as soon as they come into the room. This space between the piano and the instruments has a slightly enclosed feel to it, creating an intimate and reassuring place in this large room to begin the session together. A chair small enough for the child to sit on comfortably with his or her feet firmly on the ground is provided. The mother's (or primary carer's) chair may be a little larger but will be as near as possible to the child's size of chair so that the mother and child are sitting at the same height. Distracting objects in the room such as mirrors or toys are either covered up or completely out of reach.

This layout of the room allows me to associate musical activities with geographical locations in the room. We might play sitting on the chairs (with me sitting on the floor), for example, or sitting on the red mat in the centre of the room. At other times, we might walk around the room, or play behind the screens. The clear physical boundaries created by the chairs, the red mat and the red screens sometimes seem to help the children to settle and focus.

Beginnings and endings of sessions

At the start of the sessions the child and the mother are invited to sit on the little chairs next to the piano. I will usually be holding a guitar, and perhaps strumming a few chords to help remind the child that a music therapy session is about to begin. I make it clear that the chairs have been specially put out for the child and the mother by saying, for example, 'Danny's chair' and 'Mummy's chair'. As soon as they are both seated I will sit on the floor opposite them both so that I am at the child's eye height and start singing my 'Hello' song. If a child is reluctant to come into the room, I might go out into the waiting room with my guitar and make encouraging comments, or I might leave the door open and sit opposite the two empty chairs, quietly singing and playing the guitar.

The 'Hello' song itself serves as a theme tune which will quickly be associated with the beginning of the session. Whenever possible, I make sure I finish at least one verse of the song even if the child is struggling to move away, or trying to strum the guitar. Usually the greeting song then turns into a free strumming, vocalising and singing exchange around the open strings of the guitar.

The end of the session is always marked by a percussion exchange on the bongo drums, where I sing or chant 'Goodbye' as we're playing. For the ending, I usually make sure that we are sitting on the same chairs, in the same part of the room, as we sat on at the beginning of the session. Even very withdrawn and learning disabled children quickly associate the bongo drums with the end of the session and might point to the bongo drums or go and get them to indicate that they would like the session to end. Sometimes very anxious children will be so relieved by the sight of the bongo drums (signalling the end of the session) that they will relax for the first time at this point, and perhaps suddenly become aware of the therapist and the possibility of communication. The last few minutes of the session may then become crucial in the therapeutic relationship with these children.

Once we have finished playing together, I make it clear that the session is finished by getting up and perhaps saying 'We've finished now', and accompanying the mother and child to the door. I suggest to the child and the mother that they might like to bring a toy from the waiting room back into the room to play with while I talk to the mother. While they are out of the room I cover all the instruments up with blankets, shut the piano lid and reposition the furniture slightly so that the room looks different.

My rationale for being quite directive with my 'Hello' and 'Goodbye' activities is that any child – but particularly an isolated child with autistic spectrum disorder – is reassured by a framework surrounding an event. When first meeting a new person, children are used to being talked to and to the fact that attention is directed towards them. Even if an isolated child rejects this attention, it might be frightening suddenly to be subjected to a silent adult who waited for the child to do something before responding (Oldfield 1995).

The 'Hello' song and 'Goodbye' activity are the only two consistent things that I include in almost every session with every child. What is included in the sessions in between the 'Hello' and the 'Goodbye' is dependent on each child and may vary greatly from week to week.

Motivation

All five children described here are clearly motivated by music. Danny is very responsive to the sound of the clarinet and Leon loves making sounds himself and watching for a response. Danny can be drawn into intimate sound exchanges, and both Joseph and Leon use their whole bodies to express their immediate involvement in music making.

The children are drawn to the music in a very basic, physical way and they do not need to have any social skills or intellectual abilities to have an initial physical or emotional response.

Although this initial interest in music is a key factor for all clients receiving music therapy, it is particularly relevant to young children with autistic spectrum disorder because they are mostly not communicating easily through speech. It may well be that, for Joseph, Danny and Leon, most of the sounds they will have heard adults make around them (i.e. language) will have had little meaning. Furthermore, the language around them not only has no meaning, it is also puzzling as it obviously has meaning for other people. Quickly children with autistic spectrum disorder and little or no language skills can feel excluded from a world where everyone else can communicate through spoken language. The music making is less specific and can have similar general meanings to the child, the therapist and the mother. The music includes the child in a basic form of sound exchange. The child will no longer be the outsider he was when language was spoken. Even for children on the autistic spectrum who do have more language skills, such as John, music making can have this same equalising effect because each person can interpret the meanings of the musical sounds as he or she pleases rather than being bound by the specific meaning of language.

Another reason why music may be particularly motivating is that unlike painting, for example, or putting puzzles together which require attention and interest from the child to be successful, the music making can accompany the child even if he does not play any instruments himself or appear interested in any way. Children who are very isolated can be allowed to roam freely, but the improvised music will accompany their movements and perhaps motivate them to take an interest in where the sound is coming from. Danny, for example, gradually became aware that I was accompanying his walking movements and started emphasising his stamping. Eventually he started anticipating my responses, partly looking at me to see whether I would pick up on his walking and stamping.

Structure

For all the children described above, the clear structure of the sessions was both important and reassuring. Danny was anxious about coming into the room and even tearful at times during our first few sessions together. It seemed to be the predictable nature of the sessions that gradually enabled him to relax and enjoy the music. Leon was never anxious about coming into the room, but he needed the clear beginnings and endings with more freedom to move around in between to accept being asked to sit down briefly at the beginning and end of the session. Leon would find it difficult to remain engaged with me for very long at a time and was pleased to be able to indicate that he had had enough in a constructive way by pointing at the bongo drums which he knew would be played to close the session.

The predictable structure of familiar children's songs will often be a way of encouraging children to vocalise. Peter clearly recognised some tunes such as 'Twinkle Twinkle Little Star' and 'The Wheels on the Bus' and occasionally completed the songs by singing the last word. He could also be encouraged to maintain his interest in an activity until the songs ended. Danny associated the bells falling off his head with the song 'London Bridge is Falling Down' and would wait for the word 'down' in the song even though he used no speech himself and didn't always seem to understand spoken language.

Although I try to be flexible and will often follow the children when they initiate changes in our musical improvisations together, I will also often make a conscious effort to finish songs or musical phrases, rather than stopping midway through. I feel it can be unsettling for the children to hear too many cut-off or fragmented phrases. Instead I try to help the children to plan endings by anticipating or preparing endings to each individual activity. These endings could be prepared by saying 'one more', 'last one' or 'one two three finish'; this frequently occurs in the work with Peter.

Another structural aspect of music that seems to be particularly relevant is the ability to dwell on repetition without that repetition becoming boring or stale. Actions or phrases can be repeated with slight musical variations to maintain interest. Favourite songs can be transposed into different keys, put into minor modes or rhythmically altered to provide surprises within a safe context. Thus a familiar refrain to a song that has included unexpected changes can be seen as a welcome homecoming rather than a dull repetition.

Children on the autistic spectrum often have their own repetitive rituals, so it is not surprising that a structured, predictable framework is reassuring. Nevertheless, because the music is improvised and my musical responses will vary from week to week, I can ensure that the sessions do not become stuck or inflexible.

Balance between following and initiating

Although the contents of each of my sessions will be different every week for each child and mother, I am usually aware of alternating between following the children musically, and providing an activity where I expect the child to conform with my suggestions in some way.

With Danny, apart from being directive for a minute or two in the 'Hello' and the 'Goodbye' activities, I initially spent most of the sessions following his movements and sounds to try to gain his interest and confidence. As I got to know him, I started making suggestions to him such as offering him the cabassas to play on the mat and playing a game with bells while sitting on the chairs. However, neither of these two focused activities would have been possible with Danny had they not been interspersed with moments where he roamed freely and I followed him musically.

Playing an instrument such as the clarinet allows me to be very flexible with how much physical space I leave between myself and the child. I can also either face the child directly as I play or turn my back to the child and quite easily chase or be chased in peek-a-boo exchanges. The musical line can continue while I initiate or move away from direct eye contact. In this way the interaction can easily and quickly change from being direct or indirect communication.

In addition to interspersing non-directive interactions with the child with more directive activities, I also alternate between following the child's musical suggestions and providing my own musical material, when we are improvising together. This is clear with Peter where at times I respond musically to his expectant silence and at other times I provide my own piano structure to keep the improvisation moving.

This alternating between following and initiating is used by music therapists working with a variety of client groups. I have described this approach in more detail using the example of a case study of an older child with autistic spectrum disorder and a case study of a child with emotional difficulties (Oldfield 1995). Bean (1995) uses a similar approach with a child with cerebral palsy.

Basic exchanges

Towards the end of my work with Danny, he was just beginning to allow me to interact playfully with him. By initially following and mirroring his movements or the way he was playing an instrument, I was sometimes able to capture his attention for a second. If he then changed the way he was moving or playing and noticed that my response had also changed, we could start a basic exchange. This was clear with Danny when he first noticed that I was following his stamping movements. The advantage of improvised sound exchanges is that even very simple and basic exchanges can be repeated and varied to maintain and extend the child's interest in the exchange. Because Danny was very responsive to changes in music, his initial reaction to these changes could sometimes be channelled into brief turn taking.

One could compare Danny's progress to that of an infant whose mother meets his every need, feeding him when he is hungry and comforting him when he is in need of reassurance. When all the basic needs are met and the baby is relaxed and at ease, he will smile at his mother expecting her to smile back. I tried to follow Danny musically and to respond to any sound he made, devoting my music and my reactions entirely to his needs. When I managed to meet him musically, I would be answered by an enquiring look, or a brief musical response to my playing, moving or singing.

Leon very quickly entered into playful dialogues with me. Our exchanges increased in length and grew in intensity. Leon took turns and initiated his own ideas as well as listening and responding to my musical suggestions. In fact he was using these sound exchanges just like a baby uses babbling with his mother, imitating sounds he hears and adding new sounds with different rhythms or intonations. These babbling exchanges then lead the baby to experiment with more sounds and eventually words. Not surprisingly children with autistic spectrum disorder who use musical sound exchanges in this way often start experimenting with vocal sounds as well which then may lead to words and speech. At the end of our work together, Leon had started to add vocal sounds to his musical exchanges and started to vocalise to himself when he was playing with toys on his own or at nursery.

As babies Danny and Leon were too isolated to interact or babble with their mothers. The music therapy sessions provided an opportunity to return to pre-verbal types of communication, which may then have led to vocal exchanges and speech. The parallel between mother–baby interactions and sound exchanges in music therapy sessions has been demonstrated and explored further in two training videos (Oldfield and Cramp 1994; Oldfield et al. 1999). Many other authors and music therapists have made links between mother–baby interactions and musical exchanges.

Pavlicevic (1990, 1995, 1997) referred to the literature on mother–baby interactions to clarify the music therapist's use of clinical improvisation in music therapy. She listed key issues which she felt were essential to what she called 'direct human communication' which included 'the susceptibility of a person to the other' and 'the capacity to read the meaning of the other's acts'. She explained how 'parents respond to their infants' vocalisations as though these are communicatively meaningful, and this encourages and invites infants to develop their capacity to use their voices in a communicative sense' (Pavlicevic 1995, p.169).

Pavlicevic (1997) used the concept of 'dynamic form', which she believed corresponded to Stern's (1985) 'vitality affects' but was explicitly musical in character. She explained that, in music therapy, clinical improvisation reveals personal rather than just musical qualities about the people engaged in the playing. She wrote: 'the concept of Dynamic Form crystallises why music therapy makes therapeutic sense. By understanding the dual nature of Dynamic Form, we can draw multi-faceted meaning from the jointly created form' (p.137).

When thinking about Pavlicevic's concept of dynamic form in relation to children with autistic spectrum disorder, Robarts (1996) suggested that the dynamic musical processes in therapy can help us to understand how these children's sense of self emerges. She also wrote that:

> [By] using creatively varied structures, moods, styles of approach, the autistic child may begin to discern (aurally) the varied temporal, musical 'shapes' that underpin and organise meaningful two-way communication... How music may engage motivational states and shape experiences of relationships has been elucidated by research on the responses of normal infants and the musical behaviours of mothers when they play with their infants. (p.178)

Agrotou (1988) and Heal-Hughes (1995) compared mother–baby interactions with the client–therapist relationship in music therapy. Agrotou was particularly interested in the parallels between the baby and the client's need to withdraw after an intensive moment of interaction with the mother or the therapist. Heal-Hughes used the comparison to suggest a model of thinking about the unconscious meanings that adult learning-disabled clients are communicating in music therapy sessions.

Stewart (1996, p.22) suggested that 'the fundamental model for understanding psychodynamic music therapy events is mother–infant interaction'. The five authors I have just referred to found that the study of mother–baby interactions helped them to shed new light on their music therapy work.

However, they have not directly applied these conclusions to working jointly with mothers and young children.

The speech therapist Wendy Prevener (2000) developed a special form of what she called 'musical interaction therapy', based on the similarities of mother–infant interactions and playful musical interactive games. She worked with pre-school children with autistic spectrum disorder and their parents and gave the parents lots of ideas of musical games and interactions to develop with their children. She took further Pavlicevic's (1995) point about how parents pick up on their infants' vocalisations as though they were meaningful by suggesting to the parents of autistic spectrum children that they should join in with their children's spontaneous sounds and movements even if the children did not realise what was happening. If the child enjoyed the game, he or she might follow the parent's lead and a give-and-take conversation could develop.

It is interesting to note that all five children I described in Chapter 2 quite quickly showed a definite preference for a particular musical interaction. Joseph clearly enjoyed playing the piano and anticipating my approaching footsteps. John loved hiding behind the screen while having vocal musical dialogues with me. Leon very quickly developed a form of stick tapping exchange. Danny took a few weeks to show us that he was interested in the bells falling off his head in 'London Bridge is Falling Down'. Peter developed an interest in a variety of dramatic exchanges which, however, he would then lose interest in after several weeks and need to have replaced by a new dramatic game.

These special exchanges can be repeated and will be welcomed and recognised as favourite moments to share together. With children like Danny who are very isolated and difficult to engage, I find that it is important to find consistent moments of interest even if these moments last only a few seconds, and then insert these successful moments into weekly sessions, gradually building up a repertoire of contact moments.

I am reminded of Boxhill's 'contact song' which she writes about in her book *Music Therapy for the Developmentally Disabled* (Boxhill 1985). Obviously, it is important not to let the special activity become stereotyped or boring and to move on when necessary, but perhaps it is of particular importance to children with autistic spectrum disorder to have these reassuring and safe moments to return to within the session. For children who have little or no confidence in their abilities to communicate with the world around them, this safe and predictable moment of exchange could be seen as a kind of security blanket which then enables them to take greater risks and progress further.

Music therapy seems to be an ideal setting to explore and expand on these basic exchanges between adults and children. Janert (2001) describes these basic exchanges as 'games of pure interaction' and explains why these games are so very important and effective in establishing contact with children with autism.

Control

Many young children with autistic spectrum disorder prefer or sometimes need to be in control of situations. This wish to be in control is similar to the omnipotence that many two-year-old children would like to exercise over adults in their lives. Unlike some children with autistic spectrum disorder, most two-year-olds gradually learn that the world will not fall apart if they conform to some adult rules. For children with autistic spectrum disorder who may struggle to understand the adult world, the acceptance of outside boundaries may take much longer and be more traumatic.

Children who struggle with issues of control will sometimes have become locked in battle with adults around them. Sometimes young children with autistic spectrum disorder will have become so used to resisting any requests made of them that they no longer seem able to communicate other than through confrontational or attention-seeking behaviour. For these children it is particularly important not to allow oneself to become drawn into confrontations but to help them to re-experience positive exchanges. One way of doing this is to put the child in control of the situation in a very positive way.

In my musical interactions with children, I can very easily set up exchanges where the children can control my playing in a constructive way. Joseph's initial interest in taking part in my musical interactions was due to the fact that he realised his playing would be responded to in a predictable way. Part of Peter's excitement in his playing was due to the fact that I was following and supporting his rhythm, which he knew he was leading. Children who are distressed because they feel they have lost control can sometimes be reassured by familiar structures and tunes, in the same way that returning to a theme tune after another variation has been played can be reassuring.

In addition to reinforcing the positive sides of children being in control, I can also – as I mentioned in the section where I explored the 'balance between following and initiating' – consciously alternate between following (being controlled) and leading (controlling). For children who want to be in control for most of the time I can gradually insert small elements of direction in our musical interactions, while reverting to following again if the child starts resisting. For example, the structure of the music itself can provide a controlling element (e.g. an obvious cadence to end an improvisation) which I can manipulate without obviously being in control myself.

In my stick tapping exchanges with Leon, I echoed and followed Leon's rhythmic responses. I knew that if I strayed too far from his original suggestions, he would no longer feel in control and would lose interest in our exchange. A few months later, I was able to insert more of my own rhythmical suggestions without losing Leon's interest. However, this was a gradual process where I had to be careful to make sure that Leon always continued to have an element of control over our musical improvisation.

Peter often struggled with issues of control. He wanted to follow suggestions I made, but somehow could not give in and conform. With children like Peter I often feel that they are desperate to maintain control because being in control is the only way they can feel safe. The world is so confusing for them that to relinquish control would be frightening and unsettling. On several occasions Peter's mother, Karen, and I were able to help Peter either by giving him time and waiting until he was ready to take part, or by diverting him from the conflict he was locked in and suggesting something new and unexpected. It was interesting that Peter made a point of starting again whenever we had resolved a conflict, indicating that he was reassured by the familiar structure of the session and did not want it to be changed.

Bailey (2001) wrote her MA thesis on two children receiving individual music therapy treatment and chose to focus particularly on 'negotiating control and facilitating empowerment'. Clearly she also found the issue of control to be central to her work with children with autistic spectrum disorder.

Movement

Most young children with autistic spectrum disorder are physically able and will have reached their physical milestones such as gaining head control, sitting up and walking at expected times. It therefore seems important to allow young children with autistic spectrum disorder to move around if they want to, and enable them to use their movement skills creatively, if possible, as a means of exchange. Leon was obviously delighted that I imitated his movements. As he became engrossed in our movement exchanges he was also able to pick up and imitate my suggestions. Occasionally, Leon would be so excited by our movement exchanges that he would become over-stimulated and start running around wildly. Usually, I could predict and feel when this was starting to happen, and stop him from becoming over-aroused by slowing down the tempo of my playing or singing and moving more slowly myself.

Many young children with autistic spectrum disorder like to spend time wandering around the room, briefly looking at or touching objects they meet on the way. Using my clarinet or my voice I can wander with the children and accompany their movements. This was particularly successful with Danny. Quite often children with autistic spectrum disorder use repetitive and stereotyped movements. With some children, I find I can interact through accompanying these movements. With other children I find that they may become frantic and more isolated if I reinforce the stereotyped or repetitive movements. In this case it may be better to ignore the repetitive movements, or attempt to distract the child from making these movements, or try to modify the movements slightly.

I also find it useful to accompany a child's movements when we are playing instruments together. With Joseph, the fact that I imitated the movements he was making while playing with the reed horns gave an initially meaningless movement a creative role in the overall structure of our exchange. With both Danny and Joseph I was able to give meaning and value to a physical movement that the child offered me. The message from me to the child is that they have something of value to offer me, which will, it is hoped, also boost their feelings of self-worth.

A number of authors have written about the importance of movement in the pre-verbal communication between the infant and its mother (Bullowa 1979; Trevarthen 1979). In a research study by the movement therapist Bronwin Burford, she identified cycles of movements that occurred during interactions between mothers and babies as well as during interactions between young adults with profound learning difficulties and their carers (Burford 1988). As a movement therapist she is able to get to know and enter into the movement patterns of the autistic spectrum children she works with and establish communication in this way. It appears that by communicating with the children through movement combined with sound, I may be returning to early patterns of communication between mother and babies. Some children with autistic spectrum disorder may have missed out on these early movement exchanges with their mothers because as babies their autism prevented them from being motivated to communicate in this way. I could be re-discovering these patterns of movement exchange linked with sound in my music therapy sessions.

Linking sounds to movements naturally leads into games involving an element of excitement and surprise. Many well-known action songs such as 'Round and Round the Garden' or 'Ring a Ring of Roses' naturally link sound and movement to create a climax which young children will anticipate with excitement. Children with autistic spectrum disorder may have difficulties understanding these songs but will react to the excitement that can be generated by crescendi and accelerandi linked with movements and tailored to the musical and movement interests of each child. Children often react with delight when the adult music therapist becomes a child with them and races around the room, or jumps up and down. Leon was a little surprised that I was becoming mobile in the same way that he was. This surprise was immediately replaced with delight when he realised I had turned into a playmate.

By entering into the autistic spectrum child's world of movement I feel I am able to open new doors and provide additional possibilities for communication.

Playfulness and drama

Musical interactions encourage children to be playful and allow adults to become playful again. In some of my percussion exchanges with John, I enter into the serious, intent nature of our playful exchanges. John recognises that I am an equal partner in the play exchange and we can both enjoy the excitement of a predictable event with a musical climax. At times there can be a ritualistic and repetitive element to these exchanges and it is important to guard against the children getting stuck while helping the children to play in a serious and focused way.

It is also important for the children to see and feel adults laughing and having fun with them. Danny enjoys the fact that we can all laugh together when the bells fall off our heads.

Many young children with autistic spectrum disorder have responded well when I have pretended to go to sleep, or when I have pretended that my hand was stuck to the piano. Other children have developed their own dramatic games to suit the needs of the moment. With John, for example, he needed to have moments away from the adults as a break from intensive interactions. A game evolved where he would pretend to leave us, saying 'goodbye' and then disappearing behind some screens. After a moment or two he would re-emerge with delighted shouts of 'hello' and we would greet him dramatically as though we had not seen him for a long time.

With Peter, musical games involving drama became central to our work. He was particularly delighted with the way he was able to shoot me with the chime bells and then wake me up with the cymbal crash. Here was a way for him to be in control in a positive and playful way. It was clear that he knew this was a game the day he accidentally dropped a metal chime bell on my head while I was lying immobile on the mat with my eyes closed. When I winced with pain, his face immediately looked concerned and he said 'sorry'. I remember feeling the pain in my head at the same time as delight that he had used language and clearly understood the difference between play and reality.

Musical interactions combined with movements can very easily incorporate humour and drama, thereby once again adding to the repertoire of possibilities to communicate with children with autistic spectrum disorder.

Involving parents or primary carers

As I explained earlier, it was Anna's account of our work with John that made me realise how important it is for primary carers to be part of the music therapy sessions. In spite of the social difficulties that define the diagnosis of autistic spectrum disorder, there is evidence to suggest that young children form secure attachments with their carers (Yirmiya and Sigman 2001) and it therefore seems logical to nurture this bond by treating the young child with his or her primary caregiver wherever possible.

Many mothers enjoy being part of music therapy sessions because the work focuses on the things the child can do rather on the difficulties they may be experiencing. Many mothers will have spent at least two years of the child's life worrying about what the child was not doing and what could be wrong with their child. In some cases they will have gone from one medical practitioner to another always focusing on the delays, the odd behaviours and the child's difficulties. Although by the time I see the families they will usually already have been given a diagnosis, the children will not have been diagnosed for very long and many families might still be coming to terms with the implications of the diagnosis. Some families will have become so wrapped up in the intricacies of what is wrong with their child and the diagnostic procedure that they take some time to realise that I am not involved in assessing the child's difficulties, or in determining whether the child is on the autistic spectrum or not. For these families it is a refreshing change to focus on enjoying what their child *can* do.

Many mothers of children with autistic spectrum disorder need support and encouragement to allow them to have fun with their child. Because of the traumas they have experienced and the difficulties involved in communicating with their child, they particularly value the moments when they can play and laugh together, holding on to these moments through struggles at other moments in the week. It took a little time before Danny was able to generalise the concept of watching the bells falling off my head to watching the bells fall off his mother's head. However, Danny's mother gradually became more and more involved with her son in the sessions, using sounds carefully and sensitively to interact non-verbally with him. Playing musical instruments with their child can be a very good way of putting mothers in touch with their own need and ability to play. The mother's playfulness may easily have got lost when faced with a non-communicating baby and overwhelmed with anxiety about what was wrong with the child.

Seeing her child communicate with me through musical interactions will raise the parent's expectations of what her child can do. Knowing that her child can look up and take turns, for example, will mean that she will work hard to achieve this with her child in other settings and help that child to generalise skills acquired in music therapy sessions to other situations. Sometimes parents will pick up ideas of songs or musical activities to try out at home. Danny's mother, for example, often played the bell game with him at home, and John's mother reported that he would often hide behind the furniture at home and expect to be greeted enthusiastically when he emerged, in the same way that he hid behind the screens in the music therapy room.

At other times parents will pick up on subtle new ways of communicating with their child from watching our sound exchanges. This is again clear with Danny's mother who picked up on listening and waiting for her son in very sensitive ways.

At times a mother will be exasperated by a difficult behaviour of her child, such as a constant need to be in control or to be moving about the room. Sometimes the mother and the child will be caught up in cycles of behaviours where the child is deliberately misbehaving in order to gain a negative response from the mother. In these cases I try to help the mother focus on other positive aspects of the child and if possible attempt to turn an aspect of the difficult behaviour into something positive. For example, after Leon's mother saw our movement exchanges in the music therapy sessions she was able to be more positive about her son's constant need to be on the move. Peter's mother was proud to see her son leading the music with such enthusiasm from the drum and was reminded of a positive side to his need to be in control.

Some mothers can experience jealousy when they see their child communicating more readily with me through music than they feel they can communicate themselves. In these cases, I emphasise to the mother that it is through the music making that I am interacting with the child and try to encourage the mother to use songs or music herself. I might also try to help the mother to see the positive side of her own relationship with the child. I try to generally support and encourage mothers by helping them to feel better about their own abilities to be mothers and also by recognising how difficult it can be looking after a child with autistic spectrum disorder. Gradually, most parents understand that I am not competing with them in any way, and will trust me enough to allow themselves to play and be part of our shared sessions.

Mothers

Over the past few years of working closely with mothers (or primary carers) and young children with autistic spectrum disorder it would seem that the mothers I see fit into four broad categories.

1. MOTHERS WHO ARE SHY AND HESITANT TO BECOME INVOLVED

My approach with these mothers is usually not to give many guidelines or instructions but to wait for the questions to come from the parent. I try to give lots of support to the mother, emphasising the child's positive aspects and the role that the mother has played in enabling her child to show these positive sides. As soon as the mother does get involved in any way I will encourage her and support her as much as possible. In the end most parents will be drawn in some way by watching their child's playful interactions.

2. MOTHERS WHO TRY TO INTERACT WITH THEIR CHILD BUT ARE UNABLE TO LISTEN AND TEND TO MISMATCH MUSICALLY

These mothers either imitate precisely what the child is doing and never offer their own ideas, or give musical responses that bear no relationship to what the child has just played. Again I will try to be as sensitive as possible and certainly not criticise the mother's musical contributions. I could perhaps encourage the mother who only imitates by saying how good she is at listening to her child but how she might also like to feel free to add some of her own musical ideas. Conversely, to the mother who seems to be playing in a way unrelated to her child's playing, I might say how exciting it is to have new musical contributions but that perhaps we could also pick up on the child's ideas. Generally, however, I think these mothers pick up ways of matching from watching me interact musically with their child.

3. MOTHERS WHO ARE OVER-INVOLVED AND FIND IT HARD TO LET THEIR CHILD INITIATE ANY IDEAS

Situations with these families can be difficult because I sometimes have to decide whether to support the mother or interrupt musically to interact with and support the child. However, in most cases it is possible to do both. I try to praise and support the mother when she does wait and listen to her child, explaining how important this is, and emphasise how exciting it is that the child can make his or her own musical choices or initiate his or her own musical ideas. But I also make sure I do not forget to give as much support as possible to the mother for all the energy and commitment she is obviously putting into interacting with her child.

4. MOTHERS WHO ARE VERY SUPPORTIVE TOWARDS THEIR CHILD AND APPEAR NOT TO BE EXPERIENCING ANY DIFFICULTIES

These mothers are often full of enthusiasm and praise at the end of each music therapy session, which is of course exciting and encouraging for me. I try to help the mothers to see that the reason their child is able to be so engaged, or that the session is so positive, might well be partly because of their hard work and their commitment and dedication to their child. Sometimes these mothers have such a strong bond with their child that they take time to adjust to the fact that the child is strongly engaged with me through music making. With support, however, this is usually viewed in a positive light as the mothers will delight in seeing their child able to be involved with another adult.

It is interesting to note that when carrying out her research on music therapy with children with autistic spectrum disorder and their mothers, Warwick (1988) divided the eight mothers taking part into three broad categories. These corresponded with my categories '1', '4' and a combination of '2' and '3'. We both independently seem to have arrived at much the same conclusions.

How my approach fits in with general approaches to autism

It is now generally accepted that autistic spectrum disorder has a biological cause and is the consequence of organic dysfunction (Frith 1990, p.69). Although we do not yet know exactly what this biological cause is, we do know that there are a number of neurological dysfunctions, such as EEG abnormalities, which are more frequently found in children with autistic spectrum disorder than in the normal population. Frith concluded her chapter on the biological roots of autistic spectrum disorder by saying that:

> We should think not just about 'the' cause of autism but about a long causal chain... The hazards can be of many kinds, including faulty genes, chromosome abnormality, metabolic disorder, viral agents, immune intolerance, and anorexia from perinatal problems. (p.80)

During the 1950s, 60s and 70s, many specialists felt that autistic spectrum disorder was caused by psychodynamic conflicts between the mother and the child. Bettelheim (1967) even went so far as to suggest that children with autistic spectrum disorder should be removed from their parents.

More recently Howlin, Baron-Cohen and Hadwin (1999) have argued that children with autistic spectrum disorder have a 'Theory of Mind (ToM) deficit'. They developed special teaching methods for verbal children with autistic spectrum disorder between the ages of 4 and 13 to learn to 'Mind-Read'.

However, Richer (2001) argued that it is autistic spectrum children's failure to engage in successful interactions from an early age that accounts for their difficulties rather than a specific 'Theory of Mind' deficit. He took an ethological approach based on detailed observation of children with autistic spectrum disorder. This approach argued that:

> Autistic children had not absorbed the skills and understandings of their culture as much as other children, and...one factor constraining them was their tendency to avoid social interaction (face to face and joint attention) in which the transfer of culture took place...autistic

children were in a state of motivational conflict, in which motivation labelled avoidance or fear, was stronger than in other children and tended to inhibit other motivations such as sociability more than [in] other children. (p.24)

Later on he suggested that, because of this avoidance, autistic spectrum children's social interactions were often not reciprocal:

The result was that the interaction with autistic children often broke down and there was little negotiation of shared meanings. This breakdown constrained autistic children's acquisition of the skills of their culture: language, understanding subtle social conventions, and so on. (p.29)

He also indicated that the focus of therapy should be 'trying to create the conditions in which the early social interactions where self and other are normally integrated can take place' (p.50).

Richer's work ties in very closely with my approach. The view that I have supported from my clinical experience and my research is that young children with autistic spectrum disorder may initially respond to other people but find it difficult to maintain interest in communication. This is sometimes because the child may be actively avoiding contact. At other times, other things (such as shapes of objects, or the way objects move) appear more interesting and stimulating to the child than interacting with another person. As the child grows older, patterns of 'non-communication' become more entrenched. The child replaces the stimulation that he or she would normally get from interactions with other people with repetitive or ritualistic uses of objects. This is why I feel that it is important to intervene early to encourage and promote more communication between the primary carer and the child with autistic spectrum disorder. In this way, future isolation and autistic patterns of behaviour may be reduced. I also believe that as a music therapist I am in an ideal position to observe each individual child's patterns of communication and avoidance in great detail, thus sometimes overcoming the breakdown in communication described by Richer.

Although it is no longer believed that autistic spectrum disorder can be cured, there are quite a number of very different treatment methods and approaches that are believed to be helpful to children with this disorder, and to their families. I shall now describe a few of these treatment methods with which I feel my approach has some points in common.

The Treatment and Education of Autistic and related Communication-handicapped CHildren (TEACCH) programme is used in a number of schools in the UK. This approach was developed in the USA and is the only university-based state-wide programme mandated by law in the United States (Notomi 2001). As Storey (1998) explains, the TEACCH system sets out a clearly structured and individualised programme for each child and encourages input and liaison with the families of the children. The children are encouraged to develop an understanding of their routine for the day so that they can function independently within a familiar framework.

The Tavistock Autism Workshop Approach is informed by psychoanalysis, infant observation and infant development (Reid, Alvarez and Lee 2001). After extended therapeutic assessments, which can last around three months, some children will be offered individual psychotherapy sessions from one to five times weekly for a number of years, while the parents are offered support for themselves. Other families continue to be seen as a family group. Although this approach is obviously longer and more intense than my work, there is a similar focus on each child having unique patterns of communication and on the need to support the family. There is also a recognition of the importance of being aware of the feelings of the children, the parents and the therapist.

Janert (2001) works as a psychologist with children with autistic spectrum disorder and describes how useful interactive games are to 'reclaim non-autistic potential'. These games are based on early mother–baby interactions.

Janert as well as Zappella (2001) and Newson (2001) strongly emphasise the importance of intervening as early as possible to try to establish communication patterns between parents and young children with autistic spectrum disorder.

Caldwell (2005) outlines an 'Intensive Interactive' (II) approach that uses the body language of a child or adult to communicate with them. It is based on the infant–mother exchange of 'imitation' which is the way we learn to communicate. This is clearly very similar to my approach where I am constantly closely observing children's actions and often imitating and following. Caldwell also makes the same parallels between the work with people with autistic spectrum disorder and mother–baby interactions, as I do.

There are elements of all these treatment approaches that are relevant to my work. The TEACCH approach is similar to my work in that the predictable structure to my sessions is very important, as well as my liaison with the parents of the children. Although the Tavistock workshop approach is longer and more intense than my interventions, there is a similar focus on each child having unique patterns of communication and on the need to support the family. There is also a recognition of the importance of being aware of the feelings of the children, the parents and the therapist. Janert's (2001) interactive games have a great deal in common with the way that I work, as does Caldwell's (2005) 'Intensive Interactive' approach.

How my approach fits in with other music therapists' work

Children with autism experience difficulties in communicating. Even though music therapists use a wide range of approaches, nearly all music therapists agree that music therapy can provide the client with some form of communication. It is therefore not surprising that many music therapists have worked very successfully with children with autism and that there is a relatively wide range of literature on this subject.

General texts

Euper (1968) wrote that many authors had observed that children with autism showed an unusual interest in or ability for music. She gave examples of various exceptionally musically talented people with autism and cited a study where only one out of 30 children with autism did not show a deep interest in music (Bergman and Escola 1949; cited by Euper 1968, p.185). In my own clinical experience, I have often noticed how musically engaged children with autism were and what a musically satisfying experience it was for me to improvise with them. Only two out of around 40 children with autism that have been referred to music therapy in the past five years have not responded to treatment.

One of the first books to be written about music therapy in Great Britain described Alvin's work with autistic children in the 1950s and 60s (Alvin and Warwick 1991). This book consisted mainly of case studies, but Alvin also made some general comments about her work with this client group. These comments were very informative but tended to be general observations rather than a methodology as such. For example, she mentioned how it was important to keep some elements of the room she worked in consistent and similar, and how many of the children had an interest in the physical vibrations of the musical instruments rather than simply in the sounds themselves.

In their book *Therapy in Music for Handicapped Children*, Nordoff and Robbins (1971) included a chapter entitled 'Music therapy and personality change in autistic children'. The whole book described the Nordoff–Robbins music therapy approach which in itself consisted of a methodology which was applicable to the work they described with autistic children. However, in their chapter on children with autism they used detailed case studies to make a few points about specific music therapy approaches to children with autism. Interestingly, like Alvin, they mentioned that, with the more active children, the therapy proceeded through a certain sequence of stages. In the first stage, the child overcame initial fears and realised that the music therapy experience was a positive one. In the next stage, specific musical activities were discovered and explored; and in the final stage, the child was able to become self-expressive. Alvin also talked about three developmental phases: in the first phase the child related mainly to objects; in the second phase the child related to himself or herself and the therapist; and in the third phase the child was able to relate to other significant people in his or her life (Alvin and Warwick 1991). In my work with children with autism, I recognise some of the stages and phases described by Nordoff and Robbins and Alvin. However, I have not found that the stages are applicable to all children with autism or that the children clearly move from one phase to the next. The children often seem to fluctuate from one stage to another within sessions and may show several characteristics from different phases simultaneously.

Weber (1991) wrote a general article about music therapy as a therapeutic possibility for children with autism. She referred to various books by music therapists, including those by Alvin and Warwick (1991) and Nordoff and Robbins (1971), and then described a case study of a six-year-old girl with autism who made considerable progress through her music therapy sessions. Although this was a very general article it was of particular interest as it appeared in an arts therapies journal rather than a music therapy journal, and showed that the interest in music therapy for children with autism was spreading to other disciplines.

Toigo (1992) wrote an article in which she sought to integrate the insights of Dr Temple Grandin, who was diagnosed as having autism as a child, with current music therapy practice. The fact that music was both pleasurable and predictable was highlighted as being important. It was also interesting to note that Grandin felt that she could not follow the rhythmic 'give and take' of conversation and found it extremely difficult to synchronise her rhythms with a musical accompaniment. These points tie in very clearly with the importance of motivation and structure, which I described earlier in this chapter.

Although Gembris (1995) did not write specifically about music therapy for children with autism, he made an interesting point that the development of musical skills in young children may not be related to other developmental skills. This would explain why many children with autism who are also developmentally delayed may have quite sophisticated musical skills or be particularly responsive to various types of music making.

I will now go on to explore a wide range of case studies written by music therapists from different backgrounds with varying approaches to their work.

Case studies

Mahlberg (1973) wrote a case study reporting how music therapy had successfully increased the concentration span and non-verbal communication techniques of a six-year-old boy with autism. Clapping activities and nursery rhymes played an important part in the sessions. Many of the children I have worked with have made progress in similar areas and I have also often used 'clapping' and a wide variety of children's songs.

Birkeback and Winter (1985) used two case studies to illustrate the 'forced' and 'illusive' nature of the children's playing. They used the Nordoff–Robbins assessment scales to show that one of the children went through a period of regression at regular intervals. I have also noticed periods of withdrawal or opposition in my work with children with autism.

Gustorff and Neugebauer (1988) as well as Mengedoht (1988) wrote detailed diaries of their work with individual children with autism. In both cases the relationships that developed through music making were very intense and central to the progress that the children were able to make. Like these music therapists, I find that I usually feel very intensely involved with the children and the parents I work with. It could be that this intensity comes partly from the detailed analysis of audiotapes that these music therapists undertake of their sessions in the Nordoff–Robbins tradition. In my case the analysis of the audiotapes is replaced by detailed observations of the video-tapes of the sessions.

More recently, music therapists in the UK have written detailed case studies which show how much children receiving weekly individual music therapy sessions have benefited from the work (Bailey 2001; Howat 1995; Storey 1998; Warwick 2001; Woodward 1999). Howat and Woodward each described one case study in great depth rather than attempting to give general suggestions to music therapists working with children with autism. Nevertheless they both emphasised the importance of the emotional experience of the child with autism in music therapy sessions, implying that this could be one of the main areas to which music therapists working with this client group should pay special attention. In Warwick's case study, she felt that it was very important that the little boy she was working with could express feelings about his situation at home during music therapy sessions. However, Warwick also focuses very strongly on helping him to enjoy interacting with another person and developing his non-verbal communication skills. In a similar way to Warwick's case, for some of the children in my research project music therapy provided an important opportunity to express a variety of emotions. For others, however, the central focus was on establishing some basic forms of interaction and communication.

Storey and Bailey both included two detailed case studies in their MA theses. Storey did not describe a specific music therapy methodology although her approach evolved to fit into a special school setting. Bailey focused particularly on the issues of negotiating control and facilitating empowerment in her work with children with autism. I have also found the issue of control to be central to my work, and the structure that Bailey suggests for her music therapy sessions has some similarities with my approach.

Focused approaches

Nelson, Anderson and Gonzales (1984) suggested that music therapists working with children with autism should consider specific areas of strength and weakness for each child when planning the music therapy 'programme'. These areas were: history and responsiveness to therapy; responses to sensory stimuli; concentration; ability to cope with change; temporal perception; rhythmic movement; language; communication; and affect. I can see the relevance of each of these categories in my work with children with autism, but I would suggest that not all the categories necessarily need to be examined for each child. For example, for some children 'responses to sensory stimuli' or 'rhythmic movement' would be very important to consider, whereas for others these two areas might not be of specific interest.

Lecourt, Kim and Levinge wrote detailed case studies of their work with autistic children using psychoanalytic and psychodynamic approaches (Kim 1996; Lecourt 1991; Levinge 1990). All three of them focused on analysing and interpreting the meanings of the children's behaviours. In the music therapy sessions they used very loose structures, mainly responding and reflecting back to the children musically rather than making many musical suggestions themselves. Lecourt also described how she recorded the child's musical responses and played them back to the child. Like Lecourt, I find that it is important to listen carefully to the child and to allow myself to be led and guided by what the child does. Nevertheless, I also find that it is important to provide some leadership and structure. This may be partly because my work is much more short-term than work described by music therapists with psychoanalytic approaches, and partly because I tend to work more clearly towards helping the child and the parent progress towards clearly identified objectives. This is why I feel that it is important to provide a balance of following and leading as I have described earlier.

Other music therapists have offered possible explanations for why music therapy may be particularly effective for children with autism (Brown 1994; Robarts 1996). Some of these explanations have direct implications on the approaches that music therapists might have. For example, Robarts explained why musical improvisation was particularly good at addressing avoidance behaviours, and how the music therapist had to maintain a balance between familiar and novel approaches (Robarts 1996, p.179). Brown suggested that the fact that musical improvisations could fluctuate between fixed organisation and creativity was one of the reasons why music therapy was particularly useful when working with children with autism. This again is similar to my suggestions of following and leading.

In a later case study of a two-year piece of work with a five-year-old boy with autism, Brown (2002, p.84) described how the changes in different musical elements within the music therapy improvisations helped the boy work through his extreme need to control every aspect of his environment. Like Brown, I think that the fact that music therapy can address issues of control is of prime importance.

Schumacher (1991, 1994) writes about two stages when working as a music therapist with children with autism. In the first instance she established 'contact' with the child by putting the child's spontaneous movements, vocalisations and percussion playing into a musical context. She then established 'communication' through engaging in a form of playful exchange. I feel this describes my approach, too, and that it is useful to think about a two-stage process even though at times 'contact' and 'communication' may happen almost simultaneously. She also wrote about the importance of balancing 'nearness' and 'distance', which was very similar to my idea of alternating between following and initiating. In a later article, Schumacher and Calvet-Kruppa (1999) broke down the development of pre-verbal communication in children with autism into seven different stages. These stages ranged from 'no attempts at communication' to the child who could express an emotion and share it with another person. There are some similarities here to the Nordoff and Robbins (1977) rating scales. I recognise these different levels of non-verbal communication in the children that I work with. I also find that it is often useful to analyse very precisely in what way a child is (or is not) being communicative.

Schumacher also wrote about the importance of musical games and rhymes in her work with children with autism (Schumacher and Calvet-Kruppa 1999). As mentioned earlier in this chapter, the speech therapist Prevener (2000) developed an approach called 'Musical Interaction Therapy' which she found very successful for mothers and young children with autism. This was largely based on songs and rhymes that are sung, acted and improvised around in very flexible ways. It is encouraging to discover other therapists who also find interactive musical games useful in their work.

Tyler and Di Franco both explored case studies with children with autism to look at specific methodological issues (Di Franco 1999; Tyler 1998). Tyler showed parallels between the Laing and Winnicott attributes of the 'true and false self' and the Nordoff and Robbins ideas of the 'awakened and unawakened' music child. She explained how having both these concepts in mind helped her understanding of the therapeutic process. Although neither of the two concepts underpin all of my work, I have often felt that a child has presented me with a false smile and have wondered what was behind this mask. It is also useful to keep in mind that a new frame of reference can shed new light on the way in which a music therapist will view improvisations occurring in the sessions.

Di Franco described an approach involving three stages: sound anamnesis (assessment); observation; and clinical evaluation. At each stage he filled in complex forms asking very detailed questions about the musical and communicative behaviours of the child. I was reminded of Edith Boxhill's evaluation forms that she used with learning-disabled clients (Boxhill 1985). In both cases the questions were thought-provoking and I have frequently returned to Boxhill's evaluation forms to remind myself of the range of responses I should be aware of. Nevertheless, the danger of completing long and complex forms is that one becomes so concerned with the details of the behaviours one is looking out for that one can no longer improvise freely and creatively.

Benenzon (1982) described a detailed music therapy approach with emotionally disturbed children, some of whom were on the autistic spectrum. The therapist used a wide range of sounds, recordings and percussion instruments and often provided the opportunity for the child to play with water. In the initial period of treatment the therapist had to find 'the intermediary instrument' specific to that child which enabled the child to interact with the therapist. Although this approach is very different from mine, I do find that as I am getting to know the child I often find a particular instrument, activity or musical phrase that enables me to engage with the child. Benenzon also described treatment where he worked closely with the parents, sometimes using recordings of the parents' voices and sometimes having the parents in the room with the child. Here, there was a greater emphasis on showing the parent 'healthy' ways of interacting with the child rather than picking up on the positive sides of the parents' interactions with the children. Nevertheless, it is encouraging to find that, even in the early 1980s, Benenzon recognised how important it was to work directly with the parents.

Mahns (1988) wrote a comprehensive overview of the different approaches music therapists might have when working with children with autism. To some extent these approaches were influenced by what the therapists believed caused autism. For example, in Benenzon's (1982) work some aspects of the child were considered to be 'unborn' and the music played matched the sounds a baby might hear *in utero*. However, Mahns concluded that most music therapists did not apply a specific theory to their work but were more likely to work through the music to adapt to the needs of each individual child.

Specific approaches
Ruyters and Goh (2002) developed a special approach in their work with autistic children in which they made use of visual structure to help the child to be aware of the structure of the music therapy session. This has some similarities to the structures that I use in my work, and it is interesting that these music therapists have also found that making a clear ending to activities has helped the children to be less anxious and more independent.

Staum (2002) centred on the fact that many children with autism will sing words rather than speak them. She suggested that teachers could use songs with special words in their music classes to help children with autism to extend their vocabulary. Miller and Toca (1979) wrote a case study where a three-year-old boy with autism was helped to acquire language through an adapted form of melodic intonation therapy. In my work I have come across a number of children with autism who sing rather than speak, and Staum's and Miller and Toca's observations reinforce my conviction that many forms of vocalisations and sung words and syllables should be creatively encouraged.

Clarkson (1998) described case studies where she used 'guided imagery with music' (GIM) techniques with three youngsters with autism. This is an unusual approach with children with autism and may be more appropriate for older rather than pre-school age children.

Bryan (1989) is one of the few music therapists to have written about a music therapy group for children with autism. Her article explored how the group's music changed and gradually enabled the group to operate collectively. The methodology she described was closely linked to processes occurring in the group as a whole.

Conclusion

In the first half of this chapter I described and defined my music therapy approach. After some general comments about the layout of the room and beginnings and endings of sessions, I described eight points that I believe are crucial to my work with children with autistic spectrum disorder. These are:

- the motivating aspect of music therapy sessions
- the structure inherent in the sessions and in music making
- the balance between following and initiating
- the basic non-verbal exchanges
- the fact that children can be in control in a constructive way
- movement combined with music
- playfulness and drama in the music
- working jointly with parents.

A review of the literature in this field indicates that music therapists are convinced of the value of music therapy for children with autism. Most music therapists base their observations on one or two detailed case studies, and some have attempted to explain why music therapy is particularly effective with children with autism. A few give some suggestions regarding appropriate methodologies or approaches to this work, some of which overlap with the aspects that I feel are important in my approach.

In the chapters that follow I will come back to the eight points I have listed and describe which aspects are of particular relevance to my music therapy approaches in other clinical areas.

Music Therapy with Individual Children with Severe Physical and Mental Difficulties

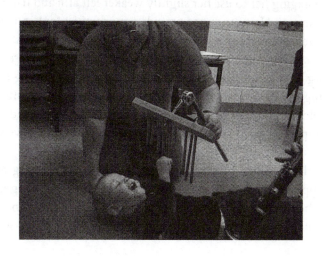

In the previous chapter I defined my specific approach with pre-school children with autistic spectrum disorder (ASD). In this chapter I focus on my work with children with severe physical and mental difficulties. I try to define what characterises my work with these children and their families and how it is different from my work with children with ASD. All the children I describe are referred to me through the Child Development Centre (CDC) and most of my work takes place at the centre at Addenbrooke's Hospital. However, I sometimes treat children from the CDC in a music therapy room at the Croft because some parents find it easier to get to and park at this location.

Three case studies

Jane and Sue

Jane was referred to music therapy by her physiotherapist when she was three years old. She attended weekly, individual music therapy sessions with her mother, Sue, at the CDC for a year.

Jane has spastic quadriplegia as a result of brain damage during birth. Both her arms and legs are affected and she has to work hard to control the use of her arms and hands. She also needs support to sit independently. She understands a lot of speech but has great difficulty producing sounds or words, and communicating is difficult.

During my work with Jane and her mother my general aims were to encourage her to overcome her physical difficulties as much as possible and to give her a means of expression and communication. More specifically I was encouraging her to use her slightly weaker left arm and hand as well as her right arm, and I was trying to provide opportunities for her to vocalise, to use her eyes to look at people or objects, and to make choices.

Because Jane struggled to sit up on her own, we started the sessions with her sitting on a foam mat on the floor, with her mother sitting behind her, supporting her as necessary. Later in the session her mother lifted her into her wheelchair and we positioned instruments on tables around her so that she could play as much as possible. We ended the sessions as we started, on the mat.

Jane clearly loved hearing the soon familiar 'Hello' song and would smile happily as soon as I strummed the first chord on the guitar. Quite quickly she would lift up her right arm to attempt to strum the strings herself. She was obviously delighted to produce a sound and would work very hard to control her movement to strum several times, even though this clearly required a big effort on her part. As she became confident using her right arm and hand I encouraged her to use her slightly weaker left arm as well, which she eventually also managed. However, it would take her time to first think about making the movement and then to control her arm sufficiently to carry through the action. I always had to be aware of being patient, listening and not rushing the musical accompaniment. I would usually improvise my singing around the pentatonic open strings of the guitar (E, A, D, G, B and E) as these were the notes that Jane was playing. This pentatonic way of improvising allowed me to sing in a very free, unstructured way, varying lengths of phrases to match up with her slow and unpredictable movements. The words I sang would be encouraging and would help to remind Jane of what she was attempting to do. Nevertheless, if I felt that Jane needed a little rest, or that a change was needed to help us to refocus, I would often insert a short energetic pentatonic tune with predictable phrases and a clear beginning and ending. This would provide a contrast to the open-ended singing.

It took Jane several months to gain enough control to hold a beater and play the drum. After much experimentation we found that she managed best when she was sitting in her wheelchair and a snare drum was placed snare side up on a low table on her right. The occupational therapist provided me with a special foam grip that I was able to slide on to the beater and make it easier for Jane to keep hold of it. Even a small tap produced a clear loud sound and Jane was delighted. However, she was also surprised by the sound she was producing and it took her a few taps every week to overcome an initial startle reflex, which would make her drop the beater. Towards the end of our year working together, Jane seemed to become more used to loud sounds and would startle less easily. She played louder, with more control, and would pick up the beater herself if she dropped it on the drum.

Jane would work incredibly hard to overcome her physical difficulties and was usually exhausted after about 15–20 minutes. At these times I would play my clarinet to her and then alternate my clarinet playing with singing about different things that Jane could look at. She understood the words I said and would slowly look around to whatever object or person I was singing about. As sessions progressed I was able to give Jane a choice of two things to look at and she was obviously pleased to be able to influence a decision in this way.

In the last few months of our work together Jane started vocalising when I played the clarinet. Her sounds seemed to fit in with the music and her gentle singing voice was very moving to hear. She would often look at her mother during these vocalisations and her mother would respond by singing back to her. It seemed to me that Jane was enjoying making music and wanting to share this enjoyment with her mother.

Jane's mother and I both felt that Jane had made considerable progress during the year of music therapy sessions. She gained greater physical control over her movements and particularly the use of her left arm and hand, and she gradually used a wider range of vocal sounds as well as making clear choices through eye pointing. In these vocalisations as well as when Jane was able to play the drum very loudly, I felt that Jane was able to use the music making to express a range of emotions which she could not easily express in other ways.

Joshua and Barry

This case study has been made into a training video (Oldfield and Nudds 2002) which is available to the general public. This video includes excerpts from weekly individual music therapy sessions over a period of 18 months when Joshua was two to three years old. You also see Joshua and his father, Barry, in physiotherapy sessions, with the specialist teacher for partially sighted children, at playgroup, at home and in the swimming pool. The video highlights the special relationship between Joshua and Barry, which is enhanced by their shared enjoyment of music making. Because of this video, unlike all the other case studies in this book, I am using original rather than changed names.

On the video, Joshua's mother, Joy, explains about the first few months of Joshua's life and his resulting difficulties:

> Joshua was born eight weeks early, due to the fact that I had pre-eclampsia. He was delivered by emergency Caesarean and everything seemed fine. He weighed 3 pounds and 7.5 ounces when he was born and the doctors hoped that at 32 weeks there wouldn't be any problems, at least they couldn't foresee any. He was on ventilators and when he was a day old he had a lung haemorrhage that caused a bleed in his brain. This is where all his problems stem from. Due to the haemorrhage to his brain, he is registered blind. Although he can see a little, his vision isn't brilliant, but hopefully this will keep improving as time goes on. He's also got hydrocephalus, so he has a shunt fitted in his

head with a tube that leads into his stomach and drains the fluid away from his brain. In addition, he has cerebral palsy, which is really the thing that's stopping him from getting on very much because, physically, he can't get about... He did have a lot of problems in hospital and anything that could go wrong did seem to go wrong at the time. I don't think that the doctors could believe how unlucky he was. Fortunately, after nine weeks we got him home and from then on he's been going from strength to strength. He's a very happy little boy and he gives us lots of pleasure... We just want him to do everything...

Because of Joshua's special needs, his parents had to adjust their lives to care for him. Barry was a postman and decided to work part-time in the early mornings so that his wife could then go to work during the day when he finished his early shift at 9am.

Barry and Joy both noticed from the time that Joshua was born that he was very responsive to sounds and music. Although his vision was very poor, he had his favourite programmes on television and responded by vocalising and moving his arms to specific songs he liked.

It was Jenny, Joshua's specialist teacher for the blind, who referred him to music therapy because she had noticed how she was able to capture his attention more easily through music and sound and because Barry and Joy had told her about his early interest in music.

In our initial music therapy assessment sessions, Joshua made it very clear from the very beginning how much he enjoyed music. As soon as I played the guitar his whole face lit up with a huge smile. His delight and excitement were wholehearted and intense. He listened intently and would sometimes join in by vocalising. He was also able to use his hands to tap or scratch percussion instruments and the guitar.

After the first few assessment sessions, Barry and I agreed that it would be useful to use the music therapy sessions to focus on:

- encouraging Joshua to overcome his physical difficulties as much as possible

- encouraging him to vocalise freely in a wide variety of ways

- enabling him to dialogue and take turns spontaneously in our musical dialogues

- giving him an opportunity to express feelings and emotions.

Joshua was beginning to use his right hand to strum as well as tap the guitar strings, and we were also trying to make him more aware of his weaker left hand by stroking it and guiding it on to percussion instruments.

During the first months, Joshua made excellent progress in his sessions. He soon became able to use his right hand not only to tap the percussion instruments more quickly and consistently, but also to strum and even pluck individual guitar strings. He particularly liked the sound of the clarinet and would often join in by vocalising. Barry also gradually became more spontaneous in his vocalisations, and he and Joshua would have wonderful singing conversations. Joshua's vocal sounds progressively became more word-like, and four months after we started sessions he surprised both of us by saying the word 'guitar'.

As Joshua grew taller it became more difficult to find ways of positioning him so that he was comfortable and able to play the instruments. On several occasions his physiotherapist, Selin, came to observe our sessions and give us advice. She showed Barry how to support Joshua in a standing position by sitting behind him and gently but firmly putting his feet on top of Joshua's feet. This arrangement meant that Joshua was able to choose to play either the drum, the cymbal or the wind chimes while keeping his head upright and watching me play the piano. We also decided to put Joshua in a variety of positions during music therapy sessions, alternating times when he had to make a big effort to sit up or stand, for example, with times when he could play instruments very easily while lying on the floor.

From Selin I learnt that she had also discovered how responsive Joshua was to sound and music and that she was using musical instruments and musical switches to motivate him in her physiotherapy sessions.

Similarly Jenny, Joshua's specialist teacher for the blind, was using musical instruments in her teaching sessions with Joshua. On the video she explained why listening was so important to Joshua:

> Actually, hearing and sound are Joshua's intact sense, his best clue to what's happening at a distance, his distance sense. Vision is not a distance sense for Joshua like it would be for everyone else. So to develop that hearing, that listening, to love using it like music helps him to do, is absolutely crucial for his understanding of the world and his general feelings of well-being.

In fact, I found that everyone who came into contact with Joshua was using sounds and music with him. At the playgroup he and Barry attended the play leaders were using glissando vocal sounds to greet him and make him giggle, and they would sing a variety of songs to help him to relax and drift off to sleep. Barry also told me that he sung songs to Joshua when he was helping him to relax in the swimming pool.

Joshua continued to make progress in music therapy sessions even after a year of regular weekly sessions. He gradually gained enough control in his right hand to hold and use a beater, which meant he could play a wider range of percussion instruments.

He was obviously listening more intently now and became aware of more complex musical phrases, waiting for the end of the phrase before responding. At times he would follow my rhythms and at other times he would initiate his own rhythmical ideas. When making music with both myself and Barry, Joshua was now taking turns and having conversations, delighting in the playful nature of these dialogues.

Joshua progressively used different consonants and a variety of vowels in his vocalisations and sound exchanges with Barry. At the same time he used more and more words and sometimes even two words such as 'more, please!'

Joshua often used the sessions to express intense excitement and delight through his playing. This made it a very exciting and positive experience for both Barry and myself to share the sessions with him. Nevertheless, Joshua would occasionally be in a quieter and more reflective mood, so Barry and I would try to respond to his playing and match whatever mood he was in through our playing.

During the 18 months that we worked together, Joshua made considerable progress both physically and in his language development. Barry also worked very hard. At first he was a little shy about singing, but then he became bolder until in later sessions he found himself almost unconsciously singing and babbling with Joshua, which then led to Joshua experimenting with speech-like sounds and using words. Joshua's interest in sounds and love of music were not confined to music therapy sessions but spilled over to all areas of his life. Everyone interacting or working with Joshua found that music was an invaluable way of getting through to him. Perhaps the most important thing was that music gave Joshua and Barry and all the other people who were involved with Joshua an opportunity for enjoyment, and a positive experience which enabled Joshua to lead a fuller life.

This is what Barry said at the end of the training video about the experience of being in music therapy sessions with Joshua:

Joshua really looked forward to going to music therapy. I enjoyed it too. I think it's done him a world of good… I wouldn't have missed it for the world. It's been really enjoyable looking after him, following what he does…and just generally being his dad.

Joshua is now attending his local village primary school. Before he started, Barry lent them the training video mentioned at the beginning of this case study so that the children could learn a little bit about Joshua. As a result Joshua was treated as a movie star when he arrived, and I understand that he continues to be a very popular little boy. I recently met him and Barry at the local supermarket and Joshua proudly introduced me to his new baby sister.

Sean and Beth

Sean was severely developmentally delayed as a result of neonatal streptococcal septicaemia and severe epilepsy. He was unable to walk and had no speech. He also had visual difficulties.

Unlike Jane and Joshua, or indeed any of the children and families described in previous chapters, I was not the first or the only music therapist to work with Sean. In fact, by the time he was five years old Sean had seen no fewer than five music therapists.

Sean was first seen by a music therapist just before his second birthday as part of the Music Therapy Home Service Project run by the local children's hospice. A music therapy student worked with Sean and his mother, Beth, in his home, for 15 sessions over a period of six months. On two occasions his father was also present, and on one occasion his sister joined in as well. She felt that the sessions with the family were productive because they were able to interact together and have a positive and enjoyable time.

Here is an excerpt from the music therapist's report (Boon 2002):

From session one, Sean was immediately involved with the musical instruments. This intense interest continued throughout and did not abate even though, at times, Sean was obviously unwell. The instruments were arranged in a semi-circle around Sean for each session and a variety offered to him throughout. Each instrument was explored and experimented with, showing intense concentration, fascination and interest. When instruments were changed, he would look for them. Sean was extremely responsive and focused during sessions. At times, he appeared to listen and be thoughtful at the different sounds each instrument produced. His playing varied from being passionate and animated to quiet and reflective.

Beth told me that when Sean first started having music therapy sessions he was having severe medical problems and sometimes up to 100 seizures a day. Neither she nor her husband thought that Sean would respond in any way. She wrote that the first music therapy session affected them both profoundly. It uplifted them and gave them hope. They were reminded that there was a little boy behind all the medical problems who could respond and connect with other people.

Sean was then referred to the CDC for further music therapy treatment. I started seeing him for regular weekly sessions when he was three-and-a-half years old, and still continue this work, two years later.

After a couple of sessions, Sean's mother and I agreed on some treatment objectives for him in music therapy sessions. These were:

- to encourage Sean to use his arms and hands in a purposeful way to play the instruments

- to encourage him to be involved in reciprocal musical exchanges with me, turn taking, responding to my musical suggestions and initiating his own

- to provide an opportunity for him to enjoy music making, and express himself, either through his playing or through vocalising

- to give Beth ideas of new ways to use music with Sean.

Like his first music therapist, I felt that Sean was drawn to and enticed by the music from the very first chord I played on the guitar. He immediately responded by tapping the wood and the strings of the guitar. Sometimes he would make a rapid scratching movement with his fingers either on the guitar or on other percussion instruments, which would produce a definite loud tap that he seemed to particularly like. He was also able to hold the bells and the tambourine. When improvising with Sean, I found that it was particularly important for me to alternate between structured melodies (such as 'What Can We Do with a Drunken Sailor?') and free fragments of pentatonic type motifs, which would fit in with his playing. I needed the freedom of the open-ended fragments in order to match his music making, but if this continued for too long I found that we would both drift and lose concentration. A well-known, strong tune with a clear structure would help us both to focus again and give our playing a clear shape.

Initially, Sean was not too sure about the new sound of the clarinet, but as sessions progressed he would smile broadly as soon as I played it. Similarly, he took a little time getting used to the piano; but once we had adjusted the height of his wheelchair so that he could have his knees under the keyboard and easily reach the keys he gradually became more and more engaged in his playing.

Sean often used a dummy, partly to prevent too much dribbling and partly to discourage him from putting his hands or other objects in his mouth. He sometimes developed nasty sores on his hands because of this habit. In music therapy sessions I found that I could remove the dummy once he was involved in the playing, but would sometimes briefly replace it if he started mouthing the instruments or putting his hands in his mouth.

Perhaps the most striking thing about making music with Sean was the intensity of his involvement. Even when he was feeling tired or unwell before the session he would always immediately immerse himself in his playing and seem to want to continue for ever. When I did end activities, he would sometimes look incredibly sad and this was very moving and sometimes distressing for me.

Another very important thing about his music making was that, after the first few months, Sean not only played more and more, but also seemed to be having the beginnings of musical conversations with me. He would play when I left a gap in my playing and appear to listen quietly during some of my playing. It was at this point that his mother asked me whether we could video his sessions because she wanted to show the sessions to his nursery teacher. She did not think his teacher would believe her if she told her how Sean was interacting with me in music therapy sessions. I refer to this session at the beginning of the introductory chapter in this book.

Beth also asked me whether there was any chance of Sean having two music therapy sessions a week. She was shy about asking me this, not wanting to be too demanding, but felt that Sean was responding more in music therapy than in any other setting and obviously wanted him to have as many opportunities as possible. Unfortunately my timetable did not make it possible for me to see him more than once a week, so after some reflection I suggested to Beth that we might try arranging for a student to see him as well as myself for weekly sessions over a period of three months. With most children and families this would not be a satisfactory arrangement as so much of the work is based on the personal relationship between the therapist and the child. Having two therapists could, for example, cause difficulties or be confusing if the child or the therapists had expectations of the sessions that could not be met. Nevertheless, in Sean's case, I felt that his deep love of and need for music was more important than a constant therapist. I also knew that I would see the student who was working with Sean on a weekly basis and that we could liaise weekly about the work we were each doing.

I also was aware that Sean had occasional one-off music therapy sessions (about three or four a year) when he visited the local children's hospice for respite care. I had had telephone conversations with his therapist at the hospice and knew that Sean had benefited greatly from these sessions and not been upset in any way.

Sean responded extremely well to having two music therapy sessions a week, so much so that the three-month work with one music therapy student was then followed by six months with another music therapy student, Sue. Sue's report on her work with Sean is included at the end of this case study.

In my sessions, I have noticed that Sean smiles and even chuckles more often and looks at me more clearly. Although he still does not want the music making to finish, he does not appear quite so sad or devastated when I take instruments away from him.

In addition to playing a wide range of percussion instruments (including the piano) with his hands, he will now sometimes briefly hold and use a beater to play a cymbal or a xylophone. He will still keep dropping the beaters he is offered, but gradually will also hold on to them and use them a little. I persist with this idea as I feel Sean would benefit from being able to play the wider range of instruments available to him if he uses beaters.

Sean's intense involvement in his playing has continued and at times our musical dialogues and exchanges seem to flow effortlessly. In spite of the severity of Sean's difficulties and the fact that he cannot communicate through words, I find that I often lose myself in our playing, particularly in our piano dialogues. Our musical exchanges take over and I will almost forget where I am or how much time has elapsed.

Sean's teacher and teaching assistant sometimes bring Sean to music therapy sessions when Beth is unavailable, because the school that Sean attends happens to be next to the music therapy room we see him in. They have both really enjoyed being part of the work. Their expectations of Sean have risen since they have seen how much he does and how well he communicates in music therapy sessions. In addition they have been able to use some of the percussion dialogues with him in the classroom. For me it has been useful to find out how Sean is outside the music therapy sessions and to be told that what is happening in the music therapy room continues to be helpful to him.

This is what Hannah, Sean's teaching assistant, wrote about the sessions:

Music does wonders for Sean. During each music therapy session, I have been able to discover different aspects of Sean's character. He responds with such great joy, enthusiasm and energy, it is a delight to watch him, especially when he reaches out for the instruments and joins in with the music therapist. I am able to see a rapport between Sean and the music therapist building up through each session, which is lovely to see. I believe music helps bring out the energy and liveliness evident in Sean's character. He is also clearly becoming more and more confident with each session.

The following was the music therapy student's report on her impressions of working with Sean.

SUE'S REPORT

When I first saw Sean I was immediately struck by the way he appeared completely disconnected from the external world, sitting slumped in his wheelchair, head down, dummy in his mouth, and focused on exploring his own fingers – seemingly unaware of any people or the environment around him. This behaviour was typical each time he arrived for music therapy over the six months I worked with him, which was my first piece of casework as a music therapy student.

My main concerns lay in his apparent frailty and complete isolation, and the challenge of how even to begin to engage him in music therapy, let alone to pursue the aims for which he had been referred – to push himself physically in different ways, to play with rather than mouth objects/instruments and to become more communicative.

It quickly became clear, however, that Sean was very responsive to music and extremely musical. Music – in this case live improvised music – completely transformed Sean's engagement with the world. In music therapy sessions, Sean became motivated to engage in a wide range of ways – whether through becoming intently absorbed and attentive, such as handling the wind chimes as I played a lyrical melody on the low flute, or through lively interaction, such as games on the ukelele or tambour, or playing the piano. His musicality was evident the whole time – with his fingers and hands constantly tapping and exploring almost any surface within reach.

I believe music therapy was extremely useful for Sean. It allowed for a mutual meeting on a non-verbal level, and gave him the chance to participate and interact with another person. For example, his delight in the ukelele, which I played to accompany my greeting song to him, generated opportunities for us to play it together, for him to explore the instrument by himself and to play the 'ukelele flying away' game (where I would gradually take it from him and move round the room before returning it to him). All these interactions allowed for turn-taking and anticipation, for Sean to develop more purposeful gripping and reaching actions, and to extend his head movements in following the sound and instrument around the room, together with many moments of eye-contact, smiling and chuckling. On one occasion, the return of the ukelele led to Sean letting loose with a stream of babbling – something which he had never done before.

The unusual situation of two different music therapists working with Sean each week required careful consideration. This approach had the advantage of further harnessing the benefits of Sean's remarkable responsiveness to and progress with music therapy. It could offer adequate time to cater for Sean's slow, deliberate, pace and need for much repetition, as well as ensuring continuity of provision when Sean was unwell and unable to attend a session. The benefits for Sean of music therapy appeared to outweigh the need for developing a relationship with simply one therapist. Indeed it could be argued that this approach had the advantage of Sean experiencing interacting with two music therapists with different personalities, musical skills and experience. Initially I felt a little uncomfortable about the imbalance of experience between myself and Amelia, who was both my lecturer and supervisor at the time. I thought I would feel the pressure of being compared, particularly as this was my first piece of casework as a music therapy student. However, my confidence increased with Amelia's positive and encouraging support, and it was quite clear that we were working in partnership for Sean's interest and benefit. This approach allowed for feeding back with each other between sessions, leading to fresh insights and thinking, and enabling us to build on approaches which were working well.

On balance, the advantages of two music therapists working with Sean appear to clearly outweigh any disadvantages. For all the reasons explored, I feel Sean should continue to have two sessions a week, and believe that another music therapy student (now that I have completed my casework), working in partnership with Amelia providing the continuity, could provide an additional valuable perspective for Sean.

It has been a delight to be and work with Sean, using a medium which he responds so well to, sharing having fun with him along with quieter time, and seeing his progress. It has been a privilege to experience the power of music therapy to begin uncovering Sean's latent capacities for communication and potential for expanding his engagement with the wider world. Indeed, the most challenging aspect about working with Sean has been the difficulty in ending different musical interactions, and to say goodbye at the end of music therapy sessions, when he is clearly so absorbed and enjoying the experience – and I am left with the feeling that in a world without time constraints, he would happily continue for hours.

When asked to write down her impressions of music therapy with Sean, his mother Beth wrote that:

> He responds to music like nothing else… Sean needs music therapy and musical games and play to achieve his potential… In the music therapy sessions it is as though a light has been switched on for Sean, allowing him to respond and enter into our world… I'm looking forward to Sean's achievements through music, throughout his life.

Reflections on these cases

Many of the points I make in Chapter 3 are relevant to working with children with severe physical and mental difficulties. In this section I focus on those aspects of the work that are different from my approach with pre-school children with ASD and their parents.

Therapist has to initiate rather than follow

The most obvious difference between the work I have just described with children with severe mental and physical difficulties and my work described earlier with children on the autistic spectrum is that the content and the structure of the sessions is more dependent on the therapist's choices. The therapist will of course take note of the child's preferences and listen to advice given by the parent, but most of the decisions regarding what should be played and where the child should be in the room initially have to be taken by the therapist. At times the therapist will have to make arbitrary choices or risk trying new ideas or instruments without being able to ask the child whether this is all right. My approach will often be to try one or two new ideas at a time while keeping what I know are favourite or reassuring and familiar activities. Sometimes I will explain to the child what I am doing even if the child does not appear to understand language. This makes it clear to the parent and to myself what I am doing, even if the child then rejects my new suggestion.

Sometimes, I will see only one or two definite responses from the child to the music I am playing or singing, or to the instruments I attempt to offer the child to play. I have to rely on what I feel is happening and, particularly at the beginning of treatment, on the reactions of the parent or the person accompanying the child. In these cases I will openly talk to the child and the parent and air my doubts and concerns as well as my positive feelings about the ways in which we are working together.

Physical limitations

Unlike children with ASD who are usually able to play a wide range of percussion and wind instruments, children with severe physical difficulties may have little or no control over their limbs. It is often challenging to think of ways in which they can contribute musically to the sessions. Sometimes I have accompanied the child's breathing or blinking and used the child's head or shoulder movements. Clark and Donna's book (1979) gives helpful guidelines for attaching beaters or instruments to various parts of the body. It is important to consider what independent movement a child has got, and then to be creative about where and how instruments can be placed or adapted to make it possible for them to play. Wind chimes or bells can be hung from stands or even the ceiling, and instruments can be placed on various tables or attached to wheelchairs. Sometimes children will be more comfortable on their mother's or the therapist's lap or may have more control playing when lying on their back or their front, or when standing in a frame.

I think children sometimes enjoy feeling sound vibrations even if they find it difficult to produce sounds themselves. I have often found it helpful to lay a child's hand on the top of a snare drum and then initiate a musical conversation through singing quite loudly just above the skin of the drum and making the snare vibrate. Even a small finger movement or a gentle kick made by the child on the snare can be heard and rewarding. In a similar way the child's palms can be curled around the top of the cabassas, and the cabassas then rotated by the therapist to produce a sound. The vibrations of the strings and the wood of the autoharp or large cymbals or gongs can also be appealing.

A number of music therapists and musicians have successfully used electronic instruments and adaptations as well as 'sound beam' with people with severe physical difficulties. I hope to learn more about these techniques in the future (Magee and Burland 2006).

Many children with severe physical difficulties are prone to infections and are more likely than other children to catch colds or viruses. Some may have to undergo frequent surgery or be regularly hospitalised. This means that the pattern of weekly music therapy sessions may often be interrupted. I am often quite surprised how quickly children like Sean and Joshua are able to remember what they were doing in music therapy sessions after a break of several weeks. Nevertheless, I always try to prepare myself for the fact that children may have regressed or lost interest after severe illnesses and prolonged absences.

Working closely with physiotherapists

With children with severe physical difficulties I have found that it is usually essential to consult and liaise with the physiotherapist regarding seating and standing positions I should be putting the child in. Joshua's physiotherapist, Selin, came to several music therapy sessions and showed Joshua's father, Barry, a special way of holding Joshua in a standing position while sitting behind him and placing his feet on top of his son's feet.

With Joshua and Jane it was important to change the children's position quite frequently as they easily became uncomfortable if they were in any one position for too long. Sean did not appear to mind remaining in his wheelchair and seemed to be in a good position to play the instruments. Sean's physiotherapist confirmed for me that I was not restricting his movements by keeping him in his wheelchair for the whole session. However, it was interesting that the music therapy student, Sue, made a point of walking around him, which he particularly enjoyed. In this way she might have been providing him with the changes of position that he was missing out on. It was interesting to find out that Selin used musical toys to distract Joshua in her physiotherapy sessions with him. So the physiotherapist was able to give me invaluable advice while picking up new musical ideas to use herself to enable Joshua to remain co-operative in the physiotherapy sessions. In a similar way, occupational therapists have often advised me on special beaters to use on the percussion instruments, or ways in which to enlarge the handles of the beaters and make them easier to grip.

Music therapy sessions can also provide an opportunity for parents or physiotherapists to move and loosen up children's over-sensitive or stiff limbs. Barry, for example, would stroke and touch Joshua's left hand while he was playing the guitar with his right hand, to try to make him more aware of his weaker left arm. He would also help Joshua to beat the drum with his right hand, which they both greatly enjoyed and which strengthened and desensitised his right wrist. Sometimes a structured and rhythmic well-known song or tune can guide the parent's movements and also make it clear when the manipulating will end. For children who may experience some discomfort when they are being moved, the fact that they know that the moving will end when the song ends may enable them to be more tolerant and patient. If, however, a child shows real signs of distress a different phrase can be improvised, slowing the movement down or stopping the song earlier.

As well as motivating children to overcome physical difficulties, music making can enable children to relax and concentrate. Sean, for example, had to control and slow down his movements, and the predictable structure of the musical phrases could help him to focus his attention and his movements on what he wanted to do. Sometimes it helps if the music therapist initially follows the rhythm of the child's movements and then builds a clear rhythmic structure around that pulse. Rising or descending vocal glissandi are also very effective ways to accompany and encourage movements.

A slower pace

The pace of the music therapy sessions with this client group is very much slower than in the previous work with boisterous children with ASD. Both Jane and Joshua frequently responded to my musical suggestions with a look or a word, but only if I gave them enough time and waited for this response. I find it is often useful to sing questions in modal keys, as it is then possible to extend phrases or repeat words for as long as is necessary while keeping the musical continuity. However, it is also useful to alternate these open-ended musical phrases with more structured definite tunes, otherwise the child and the therapist can drift off into a piece of music with no direction, and both become bored and sleepy. I also think it is important to provide variety in my music making, both by playing different instruments myself and by varying the style of my improvisations. Many children may appear quiet and frail but may enjoy loud rhythmic music more than quite gentle sounds.

Because of the slow pace of the sessions and the importance of listening and waiting silently, I sometimes have to work hard to maintain my concentration and focus. If I am not careful I sometimes find my thoughts drifting to the day's timetable or even the weekly shopping list while at the same time dreamily responding in automatic open-ended modal vocal responses. My difficulties in concentration could be partly a counter-transference phenomenon when working with children who may struggle to be motivated and to maintain concentration. The children's low levels of energy and sometimes quite passive moods can be picked up by the parents or the therapist.

On a practical note, more time may need to be allocated to individual music therapy sessions with children with severe physical problems than to sessions with ASD children. This is partly because of the slower pace of the sessions described above, and partly because it may take time to position the child in the correct ways with the most helpful tables, cushions or stands in the correct places.

Motivation

It is sometimes not easy to capture the attention of children with severe physical and mental difficulties. Moving or even attending in any way can be difficult and tiring and require a huge effort for the child. Hearing music and taking part in some way in music making can be very rewarding and will often motivate children who usually are quite passive. Children may be encouraged to look up and take an interest in the person singing, for example, and may then find it easier to maintain interest and concentration. This is somewhat similar to children on the autistic spectrum, because children with severe physical and mental difficulties will sometimes retreat into their own world. However, unlike some ASD children, children with severe physical and learning difficulties are often very communicative and can show great delight and intense joy in shared music making which can lead to very intense and moving exchanges between the therapist, the child and the parent. Jane, Joshua and Sean's faces would always light up with huge smiles as soon as I started singing the 'Hello' song, showing great potential for communication and exchange. The challenge then became to maintain the children's interest and provide a variety of ways in which musical exchanges could take place.

Vocalisations and developing words

One of the great advantages of the voice is that for some children with severe physical difficulties it is easier to use and control in some way than either their arms or legs. The urge to complete songs or phrases in songs enabled Jane and Joshua to use their voices, especially as I could make the phrases as long as necessary to give the children time to prepare and organise their vocal contribution. Linking vocal glissandi sounds to movements can also provide an additional incentive to vocalise. When a new word or sound is used it is possible to incorporate this sound or word in a wide range of musical songs and phrases, providing the repetition necessary for learning, without that repetition becoming boring or tedious. Once musical babbling exchanges are established between the child, and the parent, or the child, the parent and the therapist, these can go on for long periods, particularly if the music remains varied and interesting.

Developing a vocal repertoire may enable a child to express a wide range of emotions in ways that have not been possible previously. Joshua sometimes wanted to be quiet and wistful and share this mood with his father and myself. At other times I improvised loud energetic music to enable him to scream with laughter and share mischievous jokes with his father.

Nevertheless, some children like Sean vocalise only quite rarely. I try to provide opportunities for him to use his voice and react with delight when he does vocalise in any way. Ultimately, it remains Sean's choice whether or not to use his voice, and I do not see it as a failure on my part if he chooses not to.

Control

Children with severe physical and mental difficulties usually have very little control over any aspects of their lives and have far fewer opportunities to make choices than other children.

In music therapy sessions, although I provide plenty of encouragement, children will choose to vocalise or sing when they want to. If the children are unwilling to play in any way, I will respect this choice and perhaps play some quiet music myself, or sit quietly for a minute or two.

The excitement and intense joy that Jane, Joshua and Sean experienced when they first realised that I was responding musically to their drum tapping, guitar strumming, piano playing or vocalising was palpable and intense. I think this is because the children realised that they could be in control of the dialogue, and influence our exchange in some way.

Sometimes I make this possibility of the child being in control more obvious by jumping in the air when the drum is played, or twirling around in a circle when the tambour is tapped. In this way my dramatic movement which occurs as a result of the child's action emphasises the control the child can have over me.

Working with the parents

Most children with severe physical difficulties are recognised as needing special help at or very soon after birth. Many children will have been hospitalised for long periods and will have had prolonged life-threatening illnesses. Although the parents of these children are often exhausted and may feel low in mood, they know what their child's difficulties are and usually have some idea about what to expect in the future. They have usually at least to some extent come to terms with the fact that they have a child with special needs. This is very different from parents of children with ASD who may only recently have had a diagnosis and are still uncertain what exactly their child's difficulties are and will be.

When working with parents of children with severe physical difficulties I initially rely on the parents to advise me on how to position the child and roughly indicate to me what the child can and cannot do. Some children may have very frequent epileptic fits and I will need advice on how to react in the most appropriate way. Other children may have breathing problems and require oxygen, or will need to have help to deal with secreting too much mucus. The parents are the specialists and I am dependent on their help to look after the child.

Unlike some parents with children with ASD, there is usually a strong bond between the parent and the child and I can provide opportunities to strengthen the relationship through musical interactions and games. The parents are usually delighted to see their child having fun and able to take part in music making in some way. This is particularly so when the child does not have enough physical control to be able to easily engage in other activities such as drawing or painting.

I often find that parents of these children are very moved by watching their children enjoying music making. Like Sean's mother, they want to tell everyone about the things the child can do in music therapy sessions; and in addition to making videos of sessions, I frequently get asked whether family members or other professionals can come and observe the music therapy sessions. This is nearly always possible unless the child is unhappy having additional people in the room, and as long as the work is not disrupted by having too many or too frequent visitors. I think it is important to allow families to celebrate and enjoy the child's achievements, and many children enjoy showing off to an appreciative audience.

Other parents arrive exhausted from the on-going care they are providing for their child. One mother who was very appreciative of the work I was doing would regularly doze off in between making enthusiastic comments. At the end of the sessions she always enjoyed chatting to me about the things her daughter could do with music. She also felt relaxed enough to share with me that she had not had more than two hours' sleep at a time since her daughter had been born five years previously. For this family, as with many others, I think it is important that I provide a warm and supportive environment for both the child and the parent where listening to the parent can be as important as listening to the child.

Because I am working with both the child and the parent I have to be aware of both of their needs and sometimes sacrifice the needs of one to meet the needs of the other. For example, I might have to draw a mother back to the music making if she starts chatting to me about her holidays while I am attempting to engage them both in improvised music making. Similarly, I might have to find some toys for a child to play with if the child is attention seeking while I am reviewing the session with the parent.

Some of the children I have worked with have had life-threatening illnesses and parents have sometimes shared their concerns and fears about the child's imminent death with me. Mostly these parents focus on the 'here and now' and particularly value moments in the music therapy sessions where the child is clearly having fun and enjoying music making. Whenever possible I record these sessions on video as it is important for the parent as well as the child to know that there is a permanent record of the child and the parent's shared enjoyment. With these children I sometimes have to adjust my objectives as they become weaker and less able to hold or use the instruments. Nevertheless, the quality of the interaction between the parent and the child usually remains constant and I can continue to play music and improvise around themes and tunes I know have been favourites in the past. Other music therapists such as Griessmeier (1994) and Aasgaard (2005) have written in more depth about working with dying children and their families.

Ending my music therapy treatment

Music therapy work with children with severe physical and mental difficulties and their families is often long-term and can go on for many years. Sometimes I have found that the work has reached a plateau and become very predictable and repetitive. This might mean that it is time to stop treatment or that a few months' break will be beneficial. Occasionally, I have passed the case on to a music therapy student or a colleague and this is often beneficial for everyone. Parents may feel abandoned and let down, but I can usually help them to see that ending or having a temporary break from treatment with me may be helpful and a positive step in the long term.

In practice, my work with children and parents usually ends when the child goes to school, in the same way as it does with children with ASD. The rationale is that once the child is in school it is better for therapeutic work to take place within the school environment. The teacher responsible for the child will liaise with the music therapist, enabling progress within the classroom and the music therapy sessions to generalise from one situation to another.

In the case of Sean, however, there was no music therapy provision available within the school and the school he attended happened to be next to one of the places where I worked. As he was obviously benefiting so much from the sessions, I decided to make an exception and continue treating him. In a year's time he will move to another school and I will then be able to hand him over to another music therapist.

Sometimes I have continued to treat a child and his or her family after the child has started school and when the child is not expected to live very much longer. In these cases my past knowledge of the family has meant that it is better for me to continue work than for a new person to take over at a very traumatic time for the family.

Conclusion

This chapter shows how rewarding work with children with severe physical and mental difficulties and their families can be. Although there are many similarities between my work as a music therapist described in Chapters 2 and 3 and the work described in this chapter, there are also a number of things that are different and that characterise my work with children with severe physical and mental difficulties.

As a music therapist it is helpful to identify that there are different characteristic approaches to specific client groups. Recognising these characteristics enables the clinician to build on past experience and become more expert at approaching new cases presenting similar challenges. Nevertheless it is essential to continue to recognise that each child and family is unique and will need personal attention and consideration. Systems that have been successful in the past may be useful but will need to be thoughtfully applied to each new situation.

Chapter 5

Music Therapy with Individual Children with No Clear Diagnosis

In this chapter I describe music therapy sessions with children who do not fit neatly into the autistic spectrum disorder (ASD) diagnosis and do not have severe physical or mental difficulties, but may have some characteristics in common with the children who come under these two categories. These children are experiencing difficulties but generally have no clear diagnosis. This work occurs at the Child Development Centre, which I described in Chapter 2.

Three case studies

Lizzie

Lizzie was referred to music therapy by her speech therapist when she was five years old because her mother had told the speech therapist that she particularly enjoyed listening to tapes of songs and would hum along to familiar tunes in television programmes. She had been slow to develop speech. She needed encouragement to vocalise or use words and often seemed to find it difficult understanding what was said to her. In other ways she was very able, attending mainstream school, playing with other children and presenting no difficulties at home. There was no music therapy provision within the school that she attended. As she was already going to school and I was going to be specifically working on enabling Lizzie to use speech and vocalisations to communicate more freely and easily, we decided that I would see her on her own and feed back to her mother after every session. I initially suggested that I would work with her on a weekly basis for one term and that we would review her progress at that point.

Lizzie initially appeared to be a very serious little girl who would do anything I asked her but was quite solemn and stiff and lacked spontaneity. After discussions with her mother I decided not to put any pressure on her to speak but instead to focus on following her ideas and developing a sense of fun and play. The focus would be on non-verbal musical interactions rather than on speech.

Lizzie was quick to show that she enjoyed the familiar structure of the 'Hello' and 'Goodbye' activities, by sitting down in her usual chair and getting the guitar out for me. As she relaxed a little she joined in with the songs and started counting the guitar strings out loud. I picked up on this idea, developing the counting into a crescendo phrase with a descending pitch on the word 'six', which was sung with dramatic emphasis.

When playing the drum and the cymbal, Lizzie would gradually become more free and at ease, enjoying my accompaniment on the piano but also following my musical suggestions to play loudly or softly. With each new instrument or musical game we played together she would start off in a tense and serious way but then slowly become more and more involved, moving in a more fluid way and even laughing happily when there were musical surprises.

It was at the piano, which we played sitting side by side, that Lizzie really seemed to come into her own. She would usually suggest a song such as 'Baa Baa Black Sheep', which I would play to her and she would join in playing random notes but following the rhythm of the song. She would request the song again and again. Gradually I would vary the tune and insert surprises, which Lizzie would giggle at. If I strayed too far from the original tune, she would look at me severely and shout 'Baa baa' at me loudly. Sometimes I would pretend to go to sleep on the keyboard and Lizzie would then play loudly to wake me up. At other times Lizzie would pretend to go to sleep and laugh loudly with delight when I woke her up.

This playful approach worked very well. Lizzie became more spontaneous and communicative as sessions progressed. Over the weeks this meant that she used more and more words and her understanding of language also seemed to improve. Lizzie's mother told me that this progress was also apparent both at home and at school. At the end of our term together Lizzie's mother and I agreed that we had achieved our aims and that she no longer needed to come to music therapy sessions.

David and Pat

David was referred to music therapy by his portage home visitor. He had two initial music therapy assessment sessions and then started weekly individual music therapy sessions with his mother two months later. The family was then offered some 'circle time' sessions, which coincided with the times of the music therapy sessions from which he therefore had a break. Four months later, he resumed weekly music therapy sessions with his mother, which he has attended and continues to attend on a regular basis.

DAVID'S MOTHER'S ACCOUNT OF DAVID'S EARLY YEARS AND HOW HE IS NOW

I felt from quite early on that something was not quite right with David but I was never really sure what it was. He just didn't seem quite as aware as his older brother had been – the world seemed to be a bit of a puzzle to him. We had his hearing tested but that appeared to be all right. His motor milestones were all a bit late but still just about in the normal range – he didn't sit up properly until ten months, crawled when he was one and finally walked around 17 months. He said his first words around 13–14 months but after that his speech seemed to develop quite slowly and he didn't put any words together until after two. By the age of two he seemed a bit behind with everything – he couldn't feed himself with a spoon, crashed into everything, couldn't manage a simple puzzle or shape sorter and talked, very unclearly, in single words. I spoke to the health visitor about my concerns and was referred to a paediatrician. Since then life with David has been a constant series of appointments and assessments. We have seen speech and language therapists, a physiotherapist, occupational therapists, a clinical psychologist, an educational psychologist, paediatricians and audiologists. Everyone agrees that something is not right with David but no one really seems to know what it is or what to do about it.

So what is David like now? David is three years and eight months and quite tall for his age. He is an attractive child with blond curls and chubby features. He has problems with his gross and fine motor skills, so, for example, he has only just learned to walk downstairs holding on and he can only just scribble with a pen. He has poor 'body sense' – he finds it hard to know where his body is in space so he likes to press against things or lie on the floor. He seems to have problems planning his movements so very simple things like putting a lid on a box are difficult for him. He talks a lot and can speak in sentences but most people (except his parents and brother) can't understand him because he has difficulties with his speech sounds. Although he has come on a lot, the world still seems more of a puzzle to him than to other children of his age and he has problems with his comprehension of ideas and concepts. In spite of all this he is usually a happy and surprisingly unfrustrated child and he loves nothing better than a good laugh.

MY MUSIC THERAPY REPORT

David clearly enjoys many aspects of music and music making. He recognises and enjoys a wide variety of songs and tunes. He seems to be reassured by familiar musical phrases with clear predictable structures. He will sometimes say the words in songs if I leave long enough gaps, indicating that he has internalised and knows the text to a number of children's songs as well as songs I purposely sing to him every week in the music therapy sessions. He will also occasionally request particular songs.

David will play the guitar (strumming the strings and tapping the wood), tap a wide range of drums and tambourines and play the piano. He has just started using beaters more willingly to play the percussion instruments, although he will often hold the beaters upside down and his grasp is a little awkward. He has been willing to try the blowing instruments and seemed a little surprised when he managed to make a sound on the recorder for the first time last week.

David enjoys walking around the room and has come to expect me to sing marching songs as he does this. He also enjoys rolling around on the mat with tickling songs. He loves musical games where I hide instruments, bells fall off my head, or where his mother pretends to go to sleep and he then wakes her up with a cymbal crash.

After the first few sessions with David and Pat I decided to focus on the following aims and objectives:

- to help David to be engaged in playing with me and his mother

- to provide situations where he can give and take with me and/or his mum, dialogue and enjoy being playful

- to help him to accept direction and the structure of the session

- to support and encourage David's mother, as well as give her ideas of things to try out at home with him.

Initially, David was cautious. I felt he was interested in the instruments and in music making but needed time to trust the situation or allow me to play with him. He would often resist my suggestions and refuse to play instruments I offered him, but I did not think that he really did not want to do these things. He seemed to resist being directed in any way out of habit, or perhaps because he was not confident enough to risk trying something new. Once he had decided not to take up a suggestion, it was not helpful to persist as he would easily become very resistant, cross and stuck in a confrontational mode.

Gradually, David relaxed a little and could enjoy stamping around the room while I sung a stamping song; making suggestions for different animals in the 'Row, Row the Boat' song; and playing a few notes on the piano while I sang 'The Wheels on the Bus'.

When David returned after his circle time sessions, he remembered all his favourite activities and we soon developed a game where he would sit in a wooden trolley in the music therapy room and tell me what he was doing, or what he was imagining he was doing. He would tell me he was in the trolley, going on a picnic, to the seaside etc., and I would echo back what he had told me in a song with clear, short, repetitive phrases. I soon realised that David was expecting my answers and delighted by the predictable nature of my responses. It seemed to be very important to him that an adult was taking time to listen to his suggestions, valuing his ideas and responding in a reassuring and expected way.

Since this trolley sequence has become part of every session, David has slowly become happier, more relaxed and braver about trying out new things. He still finds it difficult at times to accept suggestions but generally conforms to the structure of the sessions. If given time, he will sometimes come back to something he has initially refused to do.

It seems to have helped to come back to some ideas every week. This has been the case with a waking up game where David's mother pretends to go to sleep and he then wakes her with a cymbal crash. Although he has often wanted to play this game, it has taken many weeks before he has understood that he needs to hit the cymbal with a stick to wake his mother up. Sometimes it is as though David's enthusiasm and excitement about an activity makes it impossible for him to organise his actions and movements to fulfil what he wants to do. In these cases it seems really important to continue to support and encourage him as he can easily lose confidence and then give up trying.

David's mother has been very good at supporting him in the music therapy sessions, sometimes interpreting for me when he has been trying to tell me something and I have not understood, and sometimes guiding and encouraging him. She has always been willing to join in our interactive games and has seemed pleased to review the sessions with me after every session.

DAVID'S MOTHER'S ACCOUNT OF THE MUSIC THERAPY SESSIONS

When David was a baby and a young toddler, I used to worry that his lack of progress was due to some neglect on my part. His brother was advanced and demanded lots of attention and David could easily get left behind. But one thing I had always done for David was sing; I sang nursery rhymes and songs to settle him at night and to entertain him in the day. He seemed soothed by the rhythm and predictability of the songs. When his portage worker suggested he could attend music therapy I felt sure David would enjoy it and I willingly took him along for an assessment just before his third birthday.

It was a bad time for David in general – although his language had progressed, his articulation was more or less impossible to understand and I think he wondered if there was any point in trying to communicate with anyone outside the immediate family. After numerous assessments he had become wary of strangers asking him to do things he couldn't and tended to rebel against requests. To be honest, I was disappointed after the first session – apart from a couple of moments where David seemed to let go and try something, he was mostly uncooperative and uninterested and there was no evidence of his love of songs and rhyme. However, we decided to stick with it. It helped me a lot to establish with Amelia what was acceptable behaviour from David, so I was no longer on edge wondering whether to intervene or not. Amelia quickly realised that David would resist any attempt to make him do something and so, within a basic structure, let him decide what he wanted to do within each session. Gradually David became more confident that he was not going to be made to do something he was not able to and began to relax and join in more each session. Music therapy became something to look forward to and enjoy and now he is always keen to go.

I think music therapy has helped David in a number of ways. I think it gave him reassurance at a particularly difficult time for him that there were people who were prepared to listen to him and try and understand what he wanted. I think it has helped him to trust other people and to dare to try new things. David has a lot of problems organising himself and his activities, but by providing a basic structure of set activities that David understands and chooses from, it has empowered him to make his own decisions and feel in control. I think it has helped him practically too; when he started he couldn't or wouldn't try to bang a drum or even shake a rattle – now he can play on the piano, the cymbal, the bongos and has even managed to make a sound on a recorder.

For me, music therapy is different because there is no pressure. David is totally accepted for what he is and we don't need to worry about why he is like what he is. It may be hard to measure, but I have seen him progress each session and it gives me confidence that he could progress in other therapies and to continue to seek out help for him. Most of all, I love to see him excited and enjoying himself and able to let go and join in.

I think David is at a stage with music therapy where new ideas and activities could be gradually introduced within the old routine and so he can start to expand his horizons. I would like to see him dare to move away from what he knows and try some new ideas himself. And his future in general? Well, like every parent, I want him to be happy.

Rose and her parents

Rose was referred to music therapy by her portage home teacher when she was three years old. The referral letter indicated that Rose was able to understand simple verbal requests and beginning to put two words together. She liked to line up her toys and follow rituals, but she also made good eye-contact and was communicative, pointing at pictures and initiating non-verbal exchanges. She would sometimes become frustrated and cross when she was not understood. She had always very much liked any recorded music and it was felt that music therapy sessions might help her in terms of her expressive language, compliance and listening and attention skills.

Right from the first music therapy assessment session, Rose smiled broadly as soon as I started playing the guitar. She looked at me directly, was obviously delighted by the music, and quickly mouthed the words to the song if I left a gap. She immediately engaged in musical dialogues where she played the drum and the cymbal and I played the piano, and she was able to follow changes of rhythm and dynamics as well as initiate her own musical ideas. Her mother and father both attended the session and were clearly delighted by their daughter's involvement and enthusiasm, indicating to me that she usually found it difficult to remain interested in any one activity for very long. We agreed to weekly music therapy sessions for one term. We agreed to use the sessions:

- to give Rose a chance to enjoy communicating with me non-verbally

- to encourage her to use her voice and vocalise in a playful way as well as to use words

- to provide an opportunity for her to play loudly and expressively.

Rose continued to be enthusiastic and communicative throughout her music therapy sessions. I always enjoyed improvising with her as she was responsive and creative and listened as well as contributing her own ideas. As sessions progressed she became playful as well and would enjoy hiding in a corner of the room while we pretended to look for her. She would give us clues as to where she was hiding by blowing the reed horns or giggling into a kazoo. She would often play the percussion instruments very loudly for several minutes at a time. At these times, I felt that she was giving vent to feelings of frustration and anger, especially as after this energetic playing she sometimes seemed more at ease and relaxed.

After a few weeks of working with Rose I became aware that she seemed to prefer holding the beaters with her right hand and would sometimes cradle her left hand in her right. She also had a slightly unusual gait and would always walk on her toes without putting her heel down. I suggested a referral to a physiotherapist, which the parents were pleased to pursue. Shortly afterwards Rose was diagnosed with mild spastic hemiplegia and given some temporary plaster casts for her feet.

After working with Rose and her parents for a term, we agreed that Rose had used the sessions well, but that for the future she would benefit more from group music therapy sessions where she could interact with other children, take turns and get used to being in a group. My colleague was running a music therapy group for pre-school children and their parents and Rose was able to join this group two months later.

Reflections on these cases

When parents know that – as Pat (David's mother) wrote – 'something is not quite right' with their child, they are anxious to find out what is wrong while at the same time continuing to hope that whatever is wrong is not serious and will eventually be put right. The longer it takes for parents to get a diagnosis the more frustrated and anxious they usually become. By the time the child is referred to music therapy, parents who have had no formal diagnosis are often quite desperate and the children may be wary of hospital visits and of being subjected to assessments. Many parents may be angry with professionals who have not provided satisfactory answers. Some may seek alternative private treatment and even travel abroad to seek specialist advice they feel is not available in the UK.

Music therapy can be helpful to the families of these children for a number of reasons. First, *music therapy is very different from any other form of treatment* that may have been offered and therefore provides the family with new hope. This is usually very positive but means that I sometimes have to help the family to have realistic expectations of what will be achieved. Although I hope to be able to help in some way, I will not perform miracles and am unlikely to resolve all the child's difficulties. Similarly, some parents latch on to their child's enthusiasm for music making, hoping that this means that the child has an unusual musical gift. Again I try to be positive while remaining realistic. I emphasise that many children are musical and that only some develop exceptional skills. I try to help the parents to focus on the enjoyment of music making rather than on the development of exceptional skills.

Second, because of the difficulties that many of these families may have experienced with diagnosis, I think *it is very important to focus on each individual child* and find out what that child's particular strengths and difficulties are and how the child responds to various aspects of music making. I try not to think about whether or not a child's patterns of communication are typically autistic, for example, but rather to reflect on what characterises that child's patterns of communication and what type of musical response will be most effective. The parent may attempt to ask me what my opinion of the child's symptoms are, but I will usually come back to that child's special musical responses rather than giving my thoughts on diagnosis.

Third, in a similar way I have to get to know each parent and *take time to gain his or her trust.* Many of the parents, like the children, will be wary of yet another professional with another opinion and more advice. Usually they know their child's strengths and difficulties extremely well and I will certainly initially seek their advice rather than giving any of my own. Many parents want to talk, be listened to and share their thoughts about their child with someone who cares and is interested. More than anything else it is the child's enjoyment of music making as well as my commitment to that child that enables the parent to trust me. Sometimes parents decide to stop music therapy treatment because another opportunity comes up that they feel they want to try out. If I think that the child is at a crucial moment in music therapy treatment I would discourage the family from stopping. In most cases, however, I have found that it is better to be relaxed about the choices parents make, respecting their choices and trying to fit in with what they feel will be of greatest benefit to the child and the family. This was the case with David who was offered a special group at the same time as music therapy after he had just started with me. When he did come back to music therapy sessions a few months later he was then able to make great progress and the treatment was also very productive for Pat, his mother. This would not have been possible if I had not had a flexible attitude, and had allowed myself to feel rejected and insisted on setting my own time scale.

Fourth, in music therapy sessions *I can focus on what the child can do* rather than on the things the child struggles with. This means that the child quickly gains confidence and parents are able to enjoy their child's successes rather than worrying about the difficulties. As parents grow to trust me they may want to discuss their feelings of anger and frustration with other professionals and I have to be careful not to become drawn into the parents' splitting of good and bad therapists. In these cases I make it clear that I am listening and empathetic, but I am there to focus on the child and the parent in music therapy rather than discussing other treatment they may have received.

Fifth, with many of the children I find that *I have to approach the difficulty they are experiencing indirectly.* Lizzie's main problem, for example, was that she was not using language. But instead of encouraging her to speak we decided to focus on encouraging her to relax, be playful and enjoy non-verbal musical exchanges. As she became more and more involved in music making, she became more communicative, vocalised freely and started talking more.

Conclusion

In the first five chapters I have described individual music therapy with 11 different children and their families. Some of the children were seen for a few months and others for several years. Some cases were described quite briefly, others at greater length with reports from parents and co-workers as well as my own. Some of the work described occurred over ten years ago and has already been written about elsewhere. Other work has been included in research investigations described at the end of this book. A number of cases are on-going at the time of writing.

After establishing eight characteristics of my work with pre-school children with autism and their parents in Chapter 3, I then attempted to draw out features that characterise my work with children with severe physical and mental difficulties in Chapter 4, and with pre-school children without clear diagnoses in Chapter 5. Many of the eight characteristics identified in Chapter 3 remain relevant and important to the cases described in Chapters 4 and 5 and to all the work described in this book. However, some aspects are different and more specific to other client groups. From a practical point of view I find it is helpful to try to balance my case load to include a variety of cases – for example, some children with ASD, some with severe physical and mental difficulties and some with uncertain diagnoses.

When my music therapy colleague and I discuss referrals, we consider the families' needs first but also what balance of clients will allow us each to work most effectively.

In spite of the differences of approaches that I have identified, interactive, improvised music making remains the central process to all these cases. Similarly, with all the families that I have described, the thinking focuses to a large extent on drawing out strengths and positive aspects of behaviour for the child and the parent.

In general terms, what I have done so far is to attempt to describe some of what I have learnt from 25 years of clinical experience. I have tried to identify patterns in my approaches to different types of children. This clarification helps me to use my clinical experience more effectively for future clients and should also be useful to other music therapists.

It is, however, important to continue to see each case as an individual with unique strengths and difficulties rather than to slot clients into categories and then apply the method relevant to that category without thinking about specific needs. Clinical experience and methodologies are invaluable, but no two children are the same. One of the most exciting aspects of my work is that each new case is a challenge from which I can continue to learn.

Chapter 6

Music Therapy Groups at the Child Development Centre

My general approach to group work is similar to individual work. The objectives for each individual within the group are non-musical and I use music or musical interactions to achieve these objectives. However, there are many aspects to group work that are very different; and because there are more people involved, there are practical considerations that have to be addressed before any group music therapy session can be organised. In this chapter I describe how I organise and prepare for these sessions as well as how the thinking behind this work differs from individual music therapy. I then describe four very different types of group I have run at the Child Development Centre (CDC).

Practicalities

The atmosphere in the room at the beginning of a session is very important as it affects how people will feel and act within the group. This is why I try to be very well prepared before children start to arrive. I usually will have chairs set out in a circle, with my chair as part of the circle half turned towards the group and half turned towards the piano. If children are in wheelchairs I will have thought about how to position them and will have prepared the necessary props for instruments. If the children are very young and we are all sitting on the floor, the mat or cushions will be ready. Often I will decide ahead of time where individual children and adults will sit. I will try to make sure children and families arrive at the same time, but if we have to wait a little bit I sit with those people who have arrived, making conversation but waiting until everyone arrives before starting the 'Hello' song. If families arrive early I ensure that there is a waiting area available for them.

I make sure I have a large enough room to accommodate all the children without people feeling crowded. This is particularly important if some or all of the children are in wheelchairs. If possible I try to run groups in rooms that are large enough to move about in, so that some time can be spent on activities involving movement and music.

I usually put the musical instruments in a corner of the room rather than in the centre of the circle, making a feature of getting and putting back instruments that we play. I try to ensure that all equipment I want to use is easily available and think ahead to any special adaptations or tables I might need for children with physical difficulties.

After the session is over I like to review the work with the adults who have been present in the group. This can be organised in a number of different ways. For example, sometimes the instruments are put away and covered up and boxes of toys are brought in to occupy the children while the adults talk. The adults might have a cup of coffee while the children have drinks and biscuits. Another possibility is that the children leave the room and do something different with other members of staff. When neither of these options is practical, the adults might come back to meet with me at a later time. As a last resort I have occasionally reviewed the session over the telephone with a key member of staff.

Group objectives

The usual reason for referring a client to group music therapy rather than individual work is because the needs of the client require a group in order to be addressed. After a term's work with Rose, for example (Chapter 5), I realised that although I had enabled her to express feelings and became more outspoken on a one-to-one basis, what she then needed was a group of children to work with in order to enable her to feel at ease taking turns, waiting and generally socialising. In some cases, therefore, I will have different aims for each individual within a group and will put the group together with the needs of the children in mind. However, if a child is being treated in a mainstream primary school and a principal objective is to help that child to socialise with other children, the other children in the group may not have any identified therapeutic needs. In this case the objectives for those children may be to have fun or to be introduced to some basic musical concepts. I do not think this is unethical as long as the music therapist is open and clear regarding what the objectives of the group are for each of the children concerned.

A music therapy group may be set up for children and parents together. In this case I will have objectives for each of the children as well as for each of the parents. Occasionally, depending on the needs of each family, the aims for the parent or the carer may take priority over the aims for the child.

As well as supporting parents, some music therapy groups may have supporting and teaching objectives for members of staff. Members of staff working with children with very severe physical and mental difficulties, for example, may welcome new ideas of things to do with the children. Sometimes I have set up small groups of three very severely physically and mentally disabled children not so much to provide opportunities for socialisation for the children, but more to support the parents of these children. In some cases the children have benefited from the fact that I was not attempting to interact with them continuously for half an hour but could give them occasional breaks while my attention was on another child in the group. For some children who struggle to focus and concentrate and only sporadically and briefly interact with the outside world, a small music therapy group can be more appropriate than intensive individual music therapy.

Teaching staff may be able to use adapted versions of some of the activities from music therapy groups in the classroom. Again, these are useful ways of using music therapy groups, but it should be clear from the outset that part of the aim is to give staff support and new ideas.

While my own children were of pre-school age I ran a music group for the village nursery for five years. The objectives of this group were to prepare the children for the social experience of school and to introduce some basic musical concepts. The way I worked and the activities I used were similar to my music therapy work with groups. However, the objectives were educational rather than therapeutic.

Occasionally I have been asked to provide one-off music therapy groups for children during clinic open days, or as part of Christmas parties, for example. While I do not feel I should spend too much of my time running these types of group, there is no harm in occasionally doing so – it may also be a good way of informing a wider staff group and families about music therapy.

Group membership

I have run both open and closed groups at the CDC. The multi-disciplinary group for pre-school children and their parents that I describe later in this chapter was an open group – individual children would leave the group (usually at the end of a school term) and new children would be referred to the group when spaces were available. When a child left the group we would prepare the group for this leaving and say goodbye to the child and the family during their last session. Before the arrival of a new child the group would be told that a new child was coming and the new family would be introduced and welcomed. The children were usually accompanied by the same adult every week, although occasionally a father or grandparent would attend in addition to, or instead of, a mother.

The assessment unit group of children that I write about in this chapter is a closed group. The same eight children from the assessment unit came every week and the group finished at the end of the term. The membership of these two different groups and the arrangements for starting and finishing work were linked to the needs of the children and the adults in the groups and to the specific purposes of the two groups. The adults who attended the closed group were the school teacher, a classroom assistant and myself. We all came to the group every week, although once or twice one of the three teaching staff was unwell and unable to attend.

Groups will be very different depending on how they are initially formed. I might, for example, select three or four children that I have been working with individually to make up a group. Although the children do not initially know each other, I put them together because I feel that the needs of the children mean that they will benefit from working together. This will be a very different experience from working with a group of children who all know each other and see each other every day because they are from the same class at school.

Group rules

With young children in particular I try to make it clear what the expectations are through modelling and encouragement rather than through stating rules verbally. Gentle physical prompts or reminders to listen tend to be more effective than lengthy verbal explanations. I try to enable children and families to take joy and pleasure in music making through showing and sharing my own enthusiasm and sense of fun.

If parents are present we will discuss together how best to address behaviour difficulties if they occur. The last resort may be for the parent or teaching staff to briefly take the child out of the group. However, wherever possible, I try to address disruptive behaviours without removing the children, even if my way of dealing with the difficulties is often to distract the child and to try to create an interest in something new or different. As soon as the child stops being disruptive and is re-engaged in some way I will praise the child, attempt to reassure him or her and show that I still care. Once the child is confident and calm again I attempt to understand what the difficulty was, usually through discussion with other adults in the group after the session. We then decide together how to approach difficulties if they occur again.

If I notice that a parent in a group seems ill-at-ease or distressed, I try to air difficulties in the general discussion time after the group. In some cases, however, particularly if I feel the parent may not wish to talk in front of other families, I will arrange for an individual time to talk to the parent.

Planning and reviewing

I will have clear individual aims for each child and parent attending my music therapy groups. These aims will be openly discussed with the parents and the staff concerned, and will be amended and changed as appropriate every few weeks or months, depending on how fast changes occur. After each group, I fill in the same on-going music therapy assessment forms (one for each child in the group) as I do for individual music therapy sessions (see Appendix 3).

If parents are involved in sessions we will usually review the session, either informally over a cup of coffee at the end of the group while the children are playing with toys, or in a slightly more structured way after the children have left the room with other staff members.

If I am running the group with other members of staff I try to prepare and review the sessions with my colleagues on a weekly basis. This will often mean meeting up after each session to review the group straight after it has taken place, and then prepare for next week's session. During these reviews there are a number of different aspects that need to be considered:

- each individual child's progress
- each parent's ways of interacting with their child
- how the children and parents worked together as a group
- how we (the staff) interacted and what roles we took within the group
- whether or not the musical activities suggested were helpful and should be repeated or modified.

Brita Schmidt (Schmidt 2004) recently wrote an MA thesis where she examined the different ways in which music therapists worked jointly with other staff. She suggested that the most satisfying type of relationship was when the music therapist worked as a co-therapist with the other member of staff where both people saw themselves as equals rather than as a specialist with a helper. It can be quite a challenge to have equal roles as the music therapist will have to be the person playing the piano, for example, and will often be leading activities musically while the co-therapist will be supporting and helping the children. As a music therapist I have often felt guilty because I had to leave my co-worker to deal with a difficult behaviour or with taking a child to the toilet while I kept the group going by continuing to play and sing. The best way of dealing with the different roles we have to play in the group and with my feelings of unease has always been to talk openly with my co-worker after each group. Although we cannot do the same things within groups we can equally share our feelings, discuss the value of what we are doing and plan future sessions together.

What musical material to use in group sessions

When working with individual children or with children with their parents, or even with pairs of children, the musical material I use is largely dependent on the individual child's musical likes and dislikes. What I do in the sessions is dictated by the child's needs and is often inspired by that child's imagination and choices. When working with groups I obviously take the musical preferences of the group into consideration and think about the needs of each person and how best to meet these needs. However, I have to choose musical material and activities to suit everyone and will often plan what I do ahead of time even if part of what I do may be spontaneous and decided on the spur of the moment.

It is useful to have a pool of activities to choose from for various groups. I find the activities I described with a colleague in the book *Pied Piper* helpful to refer to (Bean and Oldfield 2001), but I also find that there are patterns in the ways I decide what to do in groups. I will describe how I organise my musical material and activities in some detail for the second group I write about in this chapter (a 12-week group of small classes of children in assessment units). The things I do in other music therapy groups described in this book will, of course, vary, but the principles behind the structure chosen remain similar.

Four different types of group

Each group of children and families I see will be unique depending on the needs of the individuals within the group and the way in which the group evolves and takes on an identity of its own. Nevertheless, groups can be similar in size, types of client group and general objectives.

Seeing children in pairs

The smallest group that it is possible to see is a group consisting of two. Working with pairs feels very different from a group of three. There are only two types of relationship – a relationship with the other child or a relationship with the therapist. In this setting, children could become very competitive, each seeking the therapist's attention. They could also easily club together and purposefully exclude the therapist. It is important to decide ahead of time what to do if one of the children is absent. In many cases I have found that it has been beneficial to have an individual session with one of the children instead rather than cancelling the session altogether, but in some cases this might not be the case. For some children I have found that paired work is very beneficial, although it is important to be aware of the potential difficulties I have just mentioned. I will now describe a 12-week piece of work with Aaron and Cynthia.

AARON

At the beginning of the group, Aaron was five years old with a diagnosis of autistic spectrum disorder. I worked with him individually on a weekly basis for a year before starting work with him and Cynthia.

When I first started seeing Aaron, he was compliant and gentle and showed many repetitive mannerisms such as hand flapping when he was playing on his own. He seldom used language but would occasionally repeat single words he had just heard. Aaron clearly loved music and playing the instruments. He would always become more animated and energetic as he became engaged in playing. As the year progressed he became more communicative and spontaneous, started using two-word sentences and stopped repeating words in an echolalic way. I wanted to see him being as communicative and spontaneous with another child as with me, but I felt that he would be lost in a large group and needed my encouragement not to retreat into his own world or simply comply passively with any requests that were made of him.

CYNTHIA

Cynthia was four when she started work with Aaron. She had a diagnosis of Asperger's syndrome and had worked with me on a one-to-one basis for two terms before meeting Aaron.

Cynthia was an able and very chatty girl who loved telling me exactly what to do and organising different musical games for us to play together.

She was easily drawn into musical improvisations and it was through our musical interactions that I gradually enabled her to accept and even enjoy some of my suggestions, as well as insisting on directing me. The structure of the session, where we took it in turns to choose and direct activities, helped to allow her to relinquish control for some of the time. Outside music therapy sessions Cynthia was still struggling when playing with other children. If they did not immediately conform to her requests she would lose interest and go off on her own. I thought that she would benefit from some music therapy sessions with Aaron, where I might be able to help her to accept some of his ideas as well as initiate her own.

CYNTHIA AND AARON TOGETHER

For both children I felt that it was important to stick to the familiar structure of the individual music therapy sessions that they had both experienced previously. In the 'Hello' song I strongly emphasised that there were now three of us in the room and then tried to draw the children into a tapping dialogue. This started with familiar turn taking between each of the children and myself and then gradually turned into a three-way exchange. Initially the children would each quickly lose interest if I withdrew and let them play together. Gradually, however, I was able to play less and they would enjoy responding to one another.

The same phenomenon occurred with percussion and piano exchanges. I gave Aaron the cymbal, Cynthia a large drum, and I played the piano. At first, the children would follow my playing or I would purposefully follow one of the two children. Little by little it became less clear who was following who and there would be short instances where Aaron definitely followed Cynthia, and Cynthia would become excited about leading the three of us. In these improvisations I would often insert familiar tunes that I knew both children enjoyed, such as the theme tune to 'Postman Pat'. This would help them both to follow the rhythm and refocus. Towards the end of our 12 weeks together, I remember being very excited on one occasion when Aaron spontaneously started playing Cynthia's drum and she then leant over to play his cymbal. An extremely noisy improvisation followed with Cynthia playing and singing at the top of her voice and Aaron almost losing his beaters in his enthusiasm to play both instruments at once as energetically as possible.

At the piano, I would sit between the two children with Aaron on my left playing the bass and Cynthia on my right. Again we would use a mixture of known and improvised tunes and I would encourage them to interact and respond to one another musically. We also made up sung stories, particularly about a cat on one of the posters in the room. Each of us would contribute different bits to the story; Aaron's contribution would be quite concrete about the cat's size and colour and Cynthia's quite imaginative, telling me where the cat was going and who his friends were. The important thing was that we were making up a story together. Aaron was spontaneously and verbally contributing his own ideas, and Cynthia was not only giving us imaginative suggestions but accepting that both Aaron's and my ideas were part of the same story.

After 12 weeks both children had made considerable progress. Aaron was talking more. He was accepting playing with another child and sometimes showed signs of enjoying the process. On a few occasions he was even brave enough to make some suggestions and initiate ideas in both verbal and non-verbal ways. Cynthia was able to accept another child's presence and suggestions and was able to maintain her interest in playing even when she was not fully in control of the situation.

The following term Aaron successfully started attending a mainstream primary school with one-to-one support from a helper. His parents were convinced that the paired sessions with Cynthia helped him to be confident about being with other children and made his transition to school a lot smoother.

Cynthia continued to attend a small village nursery group. Two months after the music therapy work with Aaron ended, her nursery teacher fed back that although Cynthia was still finding large groups of children difficult she had now made two friends and was much less isolated than she had previously been. She was also conforming more easily to the group structure and accepting adult requests better.

Twelve-week groups of small classes of children in assessment units

These music therapy groups were run on a weekly basis for a term. Eight children, their teacher and a teaching assistant took part in the sessions. The children were four to six years old and made up an assessment unit class. Three mainstream primary schools in Cambridge had these assessment units and each took up to eight children. Most children would stay in the assessment unit only for one year but some stayed for two years. The purpose of these classes was to provide an intensive assessment and teaching environment for children for whom it was unclear what type of educational provision would be most helpful. Although the majority of the children were at least of average intelligence, many of them had difficulties with either language, concentration or antisocial behaviours, but had no clear diagnosis. It was hoped that after the children had spent a year or two in these assessment units, the teaching staff would be able to provide advice regarding future schooling. For a proportion of the children the intensive work in the assessment unit helped them sufficiently to then integrate into ordinary mainstream primary education.

The entire class and the teaching staff would come by minibus to the centre. The music therapy group lasted 45 minutes and was followed by a 15-minute review between myself and the children's teacher. During this review the children played in an outside playground.

The purpose of the music therapy group was:

- to help each of the children with one or two individual difficulties

- to provide another setting for the teaching staff to assess the nature of the children's difficulties

- to give the teaching staff ideas for musical activities to use in the classroom.

In each of the groups I found that I structured the musical activities in specific ways. The following headings should make my thinking about the overall structure of the group clearer. However, it is important to note that I did not always follow this sequence exactly even if the teacher and I had made specific plans for a particular session. If, on the day, it was not felt that the prepared ideas would be successful, we would not hesitate to suggest completely different activities on the spur of the moment.

When suggesting activities we would consider not only the individual children's needs but also how these activities fitted together. I tried to alternate between activities where everyone joined in together with moments where one or two children were playing and the others were listening. I also tried to alternate between very familiar and easy activities and more demanding and taxing tasks. In all groups, however, it was always important to think on my feet and to adapt my plans to the particular needs of the moment as well as incorporating and building on any suggestions the children made.

GREETINGS

The children and adults would come in and sit on small chairs in a large circle. The percussion instruments might be visible but would not be within immediate reach of the children. Once everyone was sitting comfortably I would take my guitar and sing my 'Hello' song directly and clearly to the group. In group work particularly I have found that it is important to sing and play with energy and confidence, even if inside I am feeling uncertain about what I am doing. If I appear to be enjoying my singing and playing this enjoyment and enthusiasm will be conveyed to the group and will be reassuring.

The same song sung at the beginning of the session every week would act as a theme tune that defined the weekly music sessions and bring the children and the adults together for a familiar event. After two or three sessions, the children and the adults would quickly pick up the words and tune of the song and join in. To provide variety I would suggest that we sung the song loudly or quietly and then fast or slow. Sometimes one child or a pair of children might be invited to sing the song on their own to the others. Alternatively one or two children might be asked to strum the guitar while the rest of us sang the song.

After the greeting I would usually incorporate some activities that involved interactions between the children.

INITIAL GROUP INTERACTIONS

A child might be given a tambourine and invited to tap his or her name on the instrument and then to tap another child's name before passing the tambourine on to that child. I would normally have modelled this by saying and tapping 'My name is Amelia and I will give the tambourine to…John,' if necessary initially passing the tambourine to another adult so that the children could learn from observing what was happening. An alternative to this idea would have been to say, 'My name is Amelia and I call John to come and get the tambourine'.

Another idea could be to tap particular likes about different children in the group – for example, 'I like John's shirt,' before passing on the instrument to John.

A large instrument such as the drum could be placed in the centre of the circle. One child would have to run up to the drum, tap a few times and then point to another child, whose turn it would be next. The challenge was for all the children to have a turn as quickly as possible without anyone speaking.

This idea could be varied by having one child point to two children who would then play together, and each point to one child when they had finished, ensuring that pairs of children rather than single children played in the middle. Many other ideas of initial group interactions could be taken from the book *Pied Piper* (Bean and Oldfield 2001).

After the greeting and an activity involving interactions within the group, I found it was important to bring the group together again by distributing instruments around and all playing together. Group playing could be tremendously exciting, but could also be chaotic and at times a little frightening. For this reason it was important to be very clear that I was in control and could stop the music if necessary. The children also needed clear boundaries around when to play and when to stop, which had to be established and redefined as necessary for each group.

DISTRIBUTING INSTRUMENTS

One quick way of doing this was to rapidly place an instrument under each child's chair, emphasising that the instrument should not be played until everyone had one. As soon as everyone had an instrument, we would practise picking up the instrument and putting it down quietly and carefully, and I would explain that when the piano music stopped instruments were to be put down quietly under the chairs. This activity could be made more dramatic by asking the children to close their eyes so that the instrument under their chair would be a surprise. Once the activity was familiar, children rather than adults could distribute the instruments.

Another way of giving out the instruments could be to ask one child to choose an instrument for another child, who then chooses an instrument for a third child, and so on. I also often used the *Pied Piper* idea where I sang the song 'Pop Goes the Weasel' and produced an instrument out of a box at each 'pop'. Whoever seemed most interested in that instrument would receive it.

ALL PLAYING TOGETHER

As soon as everyone had an instrument I would go to the piano and play, half turning towards the children as I played and encouraging everyone to join in. I would usually start with an improvised rhythmic piece of music in 4/4 time with a clear structure and predictable harmonic progressions. My purpose would be to enable everyone to take part, so the music needed to be easy to follow and engaging but not frighteningly loud or energetic. As I played I would watch the children, gauging whether my playing needed to be more or less prominent and sometimes particularly following musical suggestions made by one of the children. Sometimes I would use changes of style, rhythm or dynamics to re-engage the children, or insert a familiar tune that all the children could join in with. When I felt the children were losing interest I would bring my playing to an end with a clear predictable cadence. I would then lift my hands off the keyboard and model putting an imaginary instrument under my chair, to remind the children that this was what was expected.

There were many ways of varying the group playing. When the music stopped the children could be invited to stand up, leave their instrument under their chair and move to the seat on their left. This had the advantage of ensuring that the children had an opportunity to play a variety of instruments and did not feel hard done by if they were not initially given the instrument they most wanted.

Another variation could be that one child has a large drum and leads the playing. When the piano stops another child has a turn leading from the drum.

Group playing could also be linked to the way I played the piano. For example, half the group could play when I played at the top of the keyboard and the other half when I played at the bottom of the keyboard. When both hands played at the two ends of the instrument, the whole group would play.

Another idea could be that the children had three types of instruments such as bells, tambours and chime bars. As I played the piano I would make up a story about the autumn, for example. When I talked about the wind blowing the bells could play, when the leaves fell off the trees the chime bars could play, and when the people stamped in the puddles the tambours could play. Each different type of instrument could also be linked to a particular piece or style of music played on the piano.

MOVEMENT

The type of movement that could be incorporated into my group sessions was very dependent on the size of the room. If I had a large enough room, children would often enjoy moving freely around the room while I improvised on the piano. Sometimes it would be helpful to say to children that they were not allowed to touch each other and could move only in certain parts of the room.

Musical statues, where the children froze when the music stopped, was often popular. I would then sometimes pick out a particular child's way of moving and ask the rest of the group to dance in that particular way.

At other times I might suggest different types of movement to the children, such as marching, walking and running, depending on the types of music I was playing on the piano. Another idea might be to suggest that children move in pairs, holding hands.

The autumn improvisation described earlier could be developed through movements. The wind blowing could be shown through swaying the body and arms, the leaves falling off trees through hands and fingers moving quickly, and the stamping in puddles through stamping and jumping. Many more movement ideas can be found in *Pied Piper* (Bean and Oldfield 2001).

One more structured game that has often been very useful is the idea of making up a path with small squares of material. One child is blindfolded while another makes a stepping-stone path of about 25 pieces of material each about 30 cm square. When the blindfolded child hears a tap on the drum played by a third child, he or she makes one slow step forward. When the cymbal is played (by a fourth child) the blindfolded child must turn slowly, on the spot.

Once the movement games were finished I would often invite children to come and sit down on chairs again in twos or threes, asking some to tip-toe back, others to hop, and yet others to make giant steps, accompanying each type of movement appropriately on the piano.

ACTIVITIES INVOLVING THE GROUP AS A WHOLE

After moving around the room it was nice to have an opportunity to regroup in the circle. One idea that could be useful at this point was the song 'Willoughby Wallaby Woo' sung by Raffi (Raffi and Whiteley 1976) which involved a large stuffed soft toy elephant. The song goes 'Willoughby Wallaby Wohn…' and the children work out who 'Wohn' is. Once they have determined that it is 'John' the song continues 'an elephant sat on John…' and the elephant goes to sit on John. This activity is demonstrated, as are some of the other ideas in this chapter, in the training video I made about music therapy at the CDC (Oldfield and Cramp 1992).

Alternatively, I could ask the children to turn their chairs with their backs to the circle. I would sing a well-known song such as 'Baa Baa Black Sheep' while walking around the circle. After a phrase or two I would stop singing and put my hands on a child's shoulders to encourage him or her to fill in the gap in the tune.

This might also have been a good moment in the group for me to play a short piece to the children on the clarinet. I would often put the clarinet together in a dramatic way in front of the group, encouraging the children to guess how many pieces I would need to use, and also wet the reed and demonstrate its use. Sometimes I would alternate my playing with singing children's names, particularly if I felt children were losing focus and needed encouragement to remain engaged. In addition I often found it useful to walk around the group while I was playing the clarinet, sometimes stopping in front of a child and inviting him or her to play a dialogue with me. A theme and variations structure might have been used where the whole group clapped during the recurring theme and individual children had dialogues with me while the others listened during the variations. This activity is demonstrated on the training video I made about working with children on the autistic spectrum (Oldfield *et al.* 1999).

SMALL GROUP WORK

Four children would be invited to come to the middle of the circle and sit around a xylophone, two on each side. The 'Bs' and 'Fs' would have been removed from the instrument so that it sounded pentatonic. This also means that each child would have groups of two or three adjacent notes in front of them, which could be the notes they were allocated to play. I would accompany the xylophone playing in the same pentatonic mode on the piano and encourage single children, pairs of children or all four children to play throughout our improvisation. If the other children listening in the circle were getting bored I might suggest that they hum gently to accompany the playing. When the piece ended I encouraged applause and bowing.

Two children might be invited to improvise together on a large shared instrument such as the drum or the cymbal. I could accompany on the piano to provide support. Alternatively two children might be invited to sit back-to-back in the middle of the circle, taking turns on different instruments. Again, once the playing was finished I would initiate and encourage applause.

CLOSING ACTIVITY

At the end of the group I would try to suggest a simple idea that everyone could easily engage in. Sometimes we might sing and act out a simple action song we all knew, and I would then use the same tune to sing 'Goodbye' to the group and individual children by incorporating their names in the song. I might ask children to sit on their hands and then put their hands on their lap when they heard their name. This made it clear to everyone who was being sung goodbye to and helped me to make sure I did not forget anybody.

VIGNETTE: RACHEL

Rachel was four years old and had been at the assessment unit for one term before her class came to the CDC for weekly group music therapy sessions. She was a quiet passive little girl who tended to play in a solitary way. She was being assessed for autistic spectrum disorder although her initial tests had not shown convincing results.

Initially Rachel was very quiet in the group, watching carefully, but only speaking very briefly when spoken to and never initiating speech or making any spontaneous suggestions. After two or three sessions, as Rachel understood the structure of the session, I noticed how engaged she was in group playing, her whole body moving rhythmically to the music. After the third session her teacher commented that he had never previously seen her so involved in anything in the classroom. In the fourth session, during group playing when I was leading from the piano and all the children were playing percussion instruments, I half turned towards Rachel and started following her playing, without saying to her or the group that this was what I was doing. She continued playing happily for a while, but when she realised that I was following her she stopped playing, looking worried and embarrassed. I immediately started playing a familiar tune, which the group and Rachel followed. A week later I introduced the activity where one child played the drum, I followed on the piano and all the children followed on their instruments. After two children had had a turn I gave the drum to Rachel and, before she had a chance to worry about it, immediately went to the piano and started playing. She followed me and then I gradually allowed her to lead me. This time she kept going excitedly and eventually brought the piece to an end with a flourish. We all applauded and Rachel beamed. From this moment onwards Rachel became more and more confident in the group, often taking the lead and making suggestions. Her behaviour in the group indicated to us that she lacked confidence, but that when motivated she could be spontaneous and interactive particularly when she did not have to rely on verbal skills. A few months later she was diagnosed as having a language disorder. She was not thought to be on the autistic spectrum.

Multi-disciplinary group with pre-school children

During my last 25 years of working at the CDC, I have run various groups for pre-school children and their parents. I now describe a multi-disciplinary open group that I jointly ran with colleagues over a period of three years. This group has some points in common with a group described in an article some years ago (Oldfield and Feuerhahn 1986).

The group was run by a physiotherapist, a speech therapist and myself. It lasted 45 minutes, followed by 15 minutes when the children played with toys and the adults chatted over coffee. After the children and the parents had left, the therapists briefly discussed each child's progress and difficulties as well as how the parents were interacting with the children. As a result of this discussion, suitable group and individual activities were planned for the following session.

I ran the session, suggested activities and played instruments. The speech therapist and the physiotherapist took part with the families, sometimes making suggestions or helping individual children and parents. When we reviewed the sessions, the speech therapist would point out what aspects of communication the children were finding difficult and we would then adapt the musical interactions and activities to meet those needs. For some children who were struggling with spoken language, we composed some songs incorporating 'Makaton' signs. As Walker and Armfield (1982) and Toogood (1980) explain, this simplified version of British Sign Language is often the way to help children with language difficulties to communicate and then develop speech (see Appendix 8).

The physiotherapist would draw our attention to individual children's physical difficulties and suggest ways of positioning children next to instruments, for example, or find special grips for beaters. For some months, we had several children who lacked head control in the group and this led to the composition of several action songs (see Appendix 9). We also discussed referrals we received for the group as well as deciding when to discharge families who were attending. In some ways, I might have appeared to be the person in charge as I was leading the group. In reality, however, all the thinking behind what we were doing, and the way we were doing it, was done as a team and we all three needed each other in order to meet the needs of the families.

The children in the group all had special needs. Some had Down's syndrome and were globally delayed. Some were on the autistic spectrum but were able to tolerate being in the group. Some had cerebral palsy and needed help from their parents to sit up. The children and the parents were referred to the group usually by members of the multi-disciplinary team at the CDC because it was felt that they would benefit from the social experience, as well as our working on children's specific individual difficulties within the group.

Some parents brought their children every week, others came fortnightly, depending on the needs of the children and on how easy it was for the parents to bring them. Younger brothers and sisters were welcomed, and if older siblings were not at school for some reason they would be enlisted as helpers. The number of families that attended varied from four to ten. The ages of the referred children ranged from one to five years.

In this group I sometimes used ideas mentioned regarding the previous group, and the general way of balancing what I did was also similar. Here I describe ideas or activities that seemed specifically important to this group and that have not been mentioned before.

GREETING

The group would start with children, parents and therapists sitting in a large circle on a mat on the floor. The group always began with a 'Hello' song which I would sing to the group while accompanying myself on the guitar. Each child would then be greeted individually. I would go up to children as I sang their names and would encourage the children to strum, tap or feel the guitar. Each child's name would be repeated at least five times during individual greetings. During these exchanges the speech therapist would encourage other children to listen, watch and confirm the names. She would also encourage children to anticipate or point to the next child to be greeted. During the activity, the physiotherapist would gently ensure that children were sitting in good positions and being supported correctly by their parents.

BECOMING AWARE OF ONE ANOTHER

I would use a number of different ideas to help the children to become aware of one another in the group. For example, a small stuffed bear could be made to jump on a tambourine while I sang a song about a jumping bear. At key phrases in the song the bear jumped on to a child's lap as I sang 'the bear jumps on...Dennis!'. Most children were delighted by the jumping bear and would grasp him to make him jump back on to the tambourine. This type of activity was also good at encouraging listening, concentration and anticipation.

Some children needed to learn to listen before they could learn to recognise different people in the group. One way of doing this was to encourage the children to put their hands up in the air when the music stopped. I could also use changes of rhythm, dynamics, keys or even instruments to encourage listening and concentration.

Sometimes, even when the children were aware of one another, they still found it difficult to remember or to say each other's names. We felt that these children needed lots of time and repetition. One of the advantages of improvised songs is that names of children, colours or items of clothing can be endlessly repeated in songs without becoming boring, the changes in rhythm and melody providing variety and interest.

BUILDING UP CONFIDENCE

Even though some children in the group were aware of one another and knew each other's names, they lacked the confidence to speak in the group, take responsibility or be the centre of attention in any way. Sometimes, the structure of a song or a piece of music could help overcome this difficulty because the child would know exactly when an action was required and could prepare for that moment. In 'Pop Goes the Weasel', for example, there is plenty of time to prepare for the 'pop', once the song has started. Conversely, some children fared better without preparation. If taken by surprise, these children would do things they would have been too shy or nervous to do if they had anticipated the actions. I could do this by unexpectedly inserting a phrase into a song which required the child to do something on his or her own.

Shy children often felt supported when the whole group was singing or playing for them. For example, they would find going to the middle of the circle and bowing to the others much less frightening when everyone else was playing and singing than if everyone was waiting in silence.

In the group it was also possible to give children a sense of leadership and responsibility. For example, once the group was able to stop and start playing instruments according to my piano playing, one child could lead the group on a loud instrument such as the drum. I would follow the drummer and, since the group was used to following the piano, the drummer would in effect be controlling what the group did.

We found that the children's enthusiasm and joy was infectious. If one or two children were obviously thoroughly enjoying themselves this would usually encourage other children and parents to relax and also have fun.

THE PARENTS

Most of the parents were delighted to see their children having fun in the group and were happy to help them to take part. It helped that music making with young children was perceived to be a normal activity that all children enjoy rather than something especially designed for children with difficulties. For some parents the group was an opportunity to rediscover the enjoyment of being with and playing with their child. This enjoyment can sometimes get lost when parents spend the first years of a child's life going from specialist to specialist to determine what is wrong. Understandably they become overwhelmed by what their child cannot do. The music groups helped the parents realise and enjoy what their child *could* do.

For the parents, singing songs and playing musical games helped to break down social and age barriers. They found they could share and discuss some of their difficulties with one another. This contact often provided valuable support, particularly for young parents who were only just coming to terms with the fact that their child had special needs.

Many parents also became aware of ways in which they could use music and sound at home with their child. One parent used a clothes song at home every morning to help with dressing. Another started making dramatic pauses in her speech and exaggerating inflections in words to encourage her child to listen. One father become so enthused that he started to have guitar lessons, while a mother who had played the piano in the past started playing again. They both felt that by playing music themselves they would be able to help their children more.

VIGNETTE: CHLOE AND NEIL AND THEIR MOTHER

Chloe and Neil were three-year-old twins who were brought to the group by their mother, Maggie. The children both had cerebral palsy, with Neil more affected than Chloe. He was severely hemiplegic and struggled to walk and to use his right arm. Chloe was only mildly affected and slightly clumsy. They were both talking, Neil using clear single words and Chloe using strings of sounds, which were difficult to decipher but clearly had specific meaning to her. In spite of their difficulties the twins were a lot more able than many of the other children in the group and I quickly used Chloe as my helper, often getting her to distribute instruments or show the others what to do.

Chloe thrived in this role of responsibility but continued to remain caring and thoughtful towards her brother and other children in the group. Both she and Neil loved controlling the group by putting their hands in the air and stopping the music. Neil would work hard to stand at the drum and play drum beats that the rest of the group would follow by clapping. Both children gained huge amounts of enjoyment and confidence from the group, which then made them braver with other children in their own nursery.

Their mother was delighted to see them both having so much fun and proud of how well they were both doing. Coming to the group made her realise how much her children could do compared to other children with much greater difficulties. Up until that point she had been somewhat overwhelmed by having two children with special needs to look after.

Group of three children in wheelchairs with severe physical and mental difficulties
The three children were referred to me at the CDC by members of the multi-disciplinary team. After two individual sessions with each of the children and their mothers, I decided to invite them to work together as a small group. All three children had cerebral palsy affecting all four limbs, and two also had scoliosis of the spine. All three children were in wheelchairs. Two of the children were tube-fed and one had severe breathing problems and had to have mucus cleared from her throat once or twice every session. None of the children had any speech and it was difficult to assess their levels of comprehension. All three children had appeared to enjoy aspects of their individual music therapy sessions. The parents were very keen for the children to have music therapy treatment as they struggled to find ways of positively engaging them.

I decided that although the children might struggle to be aware of one another or interact socially they would enjoy hearing music played to all three of them in a group. They had very short attention spans, so I felt that they would get more out of many short bursts of individual attention in the group rather than longer periods of intensive individual work. I thought the parents would greatly benefit from being in a group together and be able to support one another. Finally, with a growing waiting list of children to be treated I was aware that this would be a cost-effective way of treating the three children and their parents.

The session lasted about 50 minutes, but the first ten minutes were taken up by positioning the children and placing wheelchairs and special equipment in correct places. Afterwards the parents and I chatted informally for about ten minutes and I would make a note of suggestions made for the following week.

Before starting the 'Hello' song I would make sure everyone was still and ready and build up for a clear dramatic start. This was particularly important as time might have been taken to specially position children over a wedge or in a canvas triangular chair. For all the physical needs of the children I would be guided both by the parents and by physiotherapists who would periodically visit the group and give us advice.

GREETING

After singing to the group as a whole, I would go up to individual children with my guitar. I would sing the child's name, sometimes gently touching the child's shoulder or hand, sometimes guiding the child's hand on to the guitar strings and sometimes just taking time to sing to the child and be with him or her. All the time I would work closely with the parent, asking for advice if I was not sure what would or would not be intrusive for the child. If the child made random movements I might catch a movement on the guitar and then respond to this sound. If the child made loud breathing sounds I might incorporate these into a song. I might spend about five minutes closely involved with one child before clearly bringing the playing and singing to an end and moving to the next child. If awareness was shown that I was moving on to another child, I would pick up on this and sing about the different children in the group.

GROUP PLAYING AND SOLOS

After this extended greeting I would find instruments that each child and parent could play together. This process could take time as special adaptations might be used to position instruments so that they could be played on wheelchair tables, for example, or by the child lying on the floor and using a foot. The instruments that were often very useful were the windchimes, the cabassas, ocean drums, bells and different types of tambourines, tambours and the snare drum, as already mentioned in Chapter 4. When this was possible I might bring two instruments to a child and see whether he or she could choose one of them by looking towards it. It is also useful to remember that some children like to feel the different vibrations of the instruments either near them or on different parts of their body.

Sometimes parents rather than children would do much of the playing, but if this was jointly enjoyed by both parent and child I did not feel it was a problem. Once everyone had an instrument I would go to the piano and play music for us all to play together. I would often play loud and rhythmic music with the idea of raising energy levels and creating an exciting atmosphere. This was usually very much enjoyed by children and parents, but if I noticed that anyone was clearly upset or disturbed, then I would change my way of playing. After a few minutes of playing I would make a clear ending and briefly go up to each of the children, singing to encourage him or her to play a solo. The singing would usually be a slower variation of the piece I had played on the piano. In between each child's solo I would return to the piano to play the group theme again. If children showed any signs of being aware of one another or picking up musical ideas, I would of course try to develop this by singing phrases such as 'Diana is looking at Sophie' or 'Let's all follow Sophie's beat'. It was often important to leave enough time for children to respond to one another, particularly in the expectant silences that came at the end of energetic playing.

Sometimes the children would become very vocal and noisy during sessions. I would try to go with these noises, playing and singing loudly myself, and indicating that this could be a means of making music. In most cases this opportunity to be loud and vocal for part of the session would mean that children were able to listen to the others at other times. With other similar groups, however, occasionally noisy children who were unable to stop shouting had to be reconsidered for individual rather than group sessions as they became too disruptive for the rest of the children.

MOVEMENT

The children would often enjoy being moved to music by their parents. We could have swaying music or marching music (where the parents moved the children's legs), or we sang action songs – both familiar ones and more unusual ones that I could teach the group. Action songs can be varied by introducing props such as puppets, bean-bag animals, brightly coloured scarves or pieces of material.

I also found that the children responded well when I moved around the room with my clarinet, stopping in different places and waiting for the children to notice where I was. In a similar way all three parents could move around the room to music and then they could play different-sounding instruments, one at a time when the music stopped, calling the children as they played. Activities where instruments such as the cymbal or the tambourine move around the room and in and out of the children's reach were also often very popular.

If the children are in wheelchairs and the room is large enough it may be possible to incorporate gentle or energetic wheelchair dancing where parents move the children around the room in time to the music.

Some children have a lot of involuntary movements or will repeat movements such as rocking. These movements might be turned into a game where I tried to catch a movement on an instrument or improvised around the rhythm of the rocking. Usually this would be fun and satisfying for the children, but occasionally it might lead to the children becoming frantic, increasing their movements and isolating themselves from the group. In this case I would modify my musical accompaniment or even stop attempting to join in with the child's movements in a musical way.

GIVING THE CHILDREN CONTROL

Children with severe physical and mental difficulties usually have very little control over the people around them or their lives in general. In my groups I always try to incorporate some interactions where the children are in control of what is happening, even if it is only in a small way.

One way of doing this was to encourage a child to play a drum once (with his or her arm or with a beater) and for me to stand behind the drum and jump up in the air as soon as the child had played. Usually this would produce surprise and laughter and the child would attempt to play until I had to stop jumping because I had run out of energy. A variation to this idea was for me to stand in front of a child with a tambourine held out sideways; as soon as the instrument was touched I would twirl around on the spot.

Some children particularly enjoyed the noise and chaos when an instrument fell off a table or off their lap. Occasionally children have knocked bells off wheelchair tables and enjoyed watching me catching these bells in tambourines. Of course this activity could become a little chaotic if a child repeatedly swept instruments away. If a child was trying to show us that they had had enough of an instrument it was important not to make a game of giving it back to the child.

CLOSING THE SESSION

At the end of the session, I often played my clarinet to the children and would then go up to each of them and sing 'Goodbye' using elements of the clarinet tune in my singing. Sometimes I would touch the children's hands or shoulders to make it clearer that I was saying goodbye. As well as bringing the session to a close I might sing about things that the children had done during the session.

VIGNETTE: KIRSTY AND HER MOTHER

Kirsty was four years old and had suffered severe brain damage at birth. She was unable to sit up independently or walk, and she used a wheelchair. She struggled to control her arms and legs but could sometimes direct either her arm or a leg to an instrument. She was tube-fed and often needed oxygen to help her to breathe. Her breathing frequently sounded laboured and I often felt that a lot of her energy was being used simply on trying to breathe.

In spite of all her difficulties, Kirsty would always smile broadly whenever I started playing an instrument or singing. She would watch me when I moved around the room while I played and this would help her to be aware of the other children in the room. Although there were weeks when Kirsty was too tired to move, on some occasions she would try to tap the guitar or the tambourine and particularly enjoyed playing the ocean drum with her arm and on a couple of occasions kicking it with her leg. Nevertheless, her playing was very sporadic as her movements were usually not controlled, and I would often have to wait a long time before she managed to respond to me musically.

I would often accompany Kirsty's breathing sounds vocally. I sometimes found that I could help slow her breathing a little in this way and help her to relax and be a little more in control.

Kirsty had a great sense of humour and would laugh happily when an instrument fell to the ground, or when there was a sudden unexpected change of volume or tempo in the music. Although Kirsty could not play very much in the group, she was very much liked by children and parents because of her huge sense of fun and general good humour. Mandy, her mother, was able to be proud of her daughter in the group and always liked bringing her to a session she so clearly enjoyed and where she was obviously very popular. Mandy was able to get to know the other parents in the group and share some of her difficulties and concerns with people who had had similar experiences.

Conclusion

Music is a social activity. Group singing and music making are easy ways of bringing people together. Very little conversation is necessary and people who have not met before can easily get to know each other. It is therefore not surprising that music therapy groups can be useful ways of helping children with difficulties and their parents to interact and socialise together.

In this chapter I have described four different types of group I have worked with and listed some of the musical activities I have found useful in each of these groups. It must be remembered that these activities are only a means to an end rather than an end in themselves. Often children will come up with ideas themselves and each group will develop its own way of making music spontaneously.

Chapter 7

Investigation into Music Therapy for Ten Pre-School Children with Autistic Spectrum Disorder and their Parents

Introduction

In 1999, when the opportunity arose to apply for a two- to three-year music therapy research fellowship, I knew at once that I wanted to investigate music therapy with children on the autistic spectrum. I wanted to spend time examining and describing the work that I was doing, and set up an investigation that would back up and enhance my observations. I foresaw that I would use video analyses and questionnaires to evaluate my results, as I had done in previous research. This previous research as well as some general reflections about different approaches to music therapy research will be described in a book entitled *Interactive Music Therapy in Child and Family Psychiatry* that will be published shortly after this book (Oldfield 2006). I was fortunate enough to be successful in my application for the research fellowship and the study I am about to describe formed part of my PhD thesis (Oldfield 2004).

The overall aim of the study was to more clearly define my music therapy practice with children, particularly pre-school children with autistic spectrum disorder (ASD). I felt that I was developing specific ways of working with this client group that I wanted to identify and explore. The approach I was using seemed to be successful not only for me but also for other music therapists with whom I had been involved in training, who were using all or some elements of the approach. I therefore thought it would be useful to subject my work to more rigorous analysis.

To this effect, I set up an investigation to study ten pre-school children with an a ASD each receiving weekly music therapy sessions at the Child Development Centre (CDC) over a period of two school terms. I wanted to look at whether changes were occurring in the children and whether there were similarities in these changes across the children. I was also interested in finding out how I distributed my time playing different instruments and using movement in the music therapy sessions, and how this varied across the children. As so much of my work relies on spontaneous, intuitive musical improvisations, video analysis was used to look more objectively at what I was doing with the children.

In addition, I was interested in looking at how the parents benefited from being in the music therapy sessions with their children. Parents of young children with ASD were in particular need of support and encouragement. I therefore wanted to use video analysis to look at whether the patterns of communication between the parent and the child changed during treatment and what these changes seemed to be associated with. I was interested in finding out whether there were similarities and differences between the ways the ten different parents related to their children. I was also curious about how the parents felt about their children and whether these feelings changed in any way as a result of the music therapy intervention.

At the beginning of the project I decided that I wanted to use some of the research funding I had received from the Music Therapy Charity to employ a part-time research assistant. Emma Davies (née Carter) was therefore employed partly as a music therapist at the Croft and at the CDC to replace my clinical hours and give me time to do the research, and partly as my research assistant. Her main jobs as research assistant in this investigation were:

- to interview the parents before and after music therapy treatment
- to videotape the music therapy sessions
- to analyse all the videotapes of the music therapy sessions (after I had given her exact instructions about which codes to use for each child and parent)
- to help collect and count the data from the video analysis.

Literature review

Evers (1992) conducted a survey to find out how well accepted music therapy was by paediatricians and child psychiatrists in the Federal Republic of Germany. Not surprisingly the willingness to refer a child to music therapy was related to the clinicians' knowledge of music therapy and also to their own personal interest in music making and music listening. Overall, the statistics are encouraging and show that 14.5 per cent of the paediatricians and 56 per cent of the child psychiatrists who took part in the survey recommended music therapy as a form of treatment for children with ASD. Nevertheless, most of the clinicians also indicated that there was a need for more research in this area.

Although most of the literature in this area tends to be descriptive, a few music therapists have set up research projects. As early as 1969, Stevens and Clark looked at how relationships, communication skills and motivation improved in five children with ASD receiving weekly individual music therapy sessions over a period of 18 weeks. Significant improvements were made, but the authors felt that the rating scales they used were too imprecise to assess some of the more intricate behaviour changes.

Burday (1995) looked at whether ten children with ASD would learn signs and speech better if the words were taught with music rather than with a rhythm. Results were positive, indicating that music could help the children to learn.

Edgerton (1994) looked at ten children with ASD between the ages of six and nine who had individual music therapy sessions. The purpose of this study was to examine the effects of improvisational music therapy upon the communicative behaviours of the children. She asked specific questions regarding numbers and types of communicative behaviours in the children as music therapy sessions progressed, as well as comparing the children's scores with ratings made by parents and teachers. To measure communicative behaviours she devised an original checklist – Checklist of Communicative Responses/Acts Score Sheet (CRASS) – based on items from numerous rating scales and assessments for musical communicativeness, ASD and communication scales. Each of the sessions was videotaped and ten-minute excerpts were randomly selected for analysis. Two observers independently viewed the excerpts, recording the communicative behaviours of each child, using the CRASS. Edgerton used a reversal design consisting of (a) intervention, (b) in session six, withdrawal of intervention, and (c) reintroduction of intervention. Withdrawal of intervention in session six consisted of playing and singing pre-composed music as opposed to improvised music. She found that music therapy was effective in increasing ASD children's communication over a period of ten weekly individual sessions. She also found that communicative behaviours decreased in session six when the music therapist used pre-composed songs instead of improvised music. When comparing four musical modalities (tempo, rhythm, structure/form and pitch) across the ten children, she noted that the scores for tempo increased most, with rhythm second and structure/form third.

In 1986 Warwick teamed up with the research psychologist Muller to investigate ten children with ASD receiving music therapy partly with their mothers and partly without (Warwick 1988, 1995). It was hypothesised that music therapy would be shown to have positive effects on the children, that these positive effects would generalise to situations outside music therapy sessions, and that the mothers' attitude towards the children would become more positive and facilitate the generalisation process. The ten children were divided into two groups. The first group received individual weekly music therapy sessions for a term without their mothers, while the second group received treatment with their mothers. The groups then crossed over for a further term. Treatment occurred in the children's homes. The mothers were asked to play with their children for 15 minutes before and after each music therapy session. Warwick (1995) indicated that this investigation showed that the mothers' perceptions of their children became more positive. She also suggested that the parents could be divided into three different groups, which I have referred to in Chapter 3.

Plahl undertook a detailed investigation where she studied 12 young multiply-disabled children between the ages of two and six years (some of whom were on the autistic spectrum) each receiving ten music therapy sessions (Plahl 2000). She hypothesised that the children would make progress in seven different areas: pre-verbal communication, concentration, communicative contributions, intentional communicative participation, communicative reactions, dialogues, and communicative expression. She measured results by using detailed video analyses (she developed her own video analysis form, 'Kamuthe'), music therapy reports, rating scales, psychological tests and interviews with parents. The investigation showed that progress was achieved by the children in a number of areas, such as pre-verbal communication and concentration.

All of these investigations had positive outcomes and showed that music therapy was effective. Edgerton and Plahl used well-defined music therapy approaches in their research. Edgerton used a Nordoff and Robbins approach and Plahl studied music therapists using the Orff approach. The successful outcome of their investigations confirms both Edgerton and Plahl's belief in the music therapy systems they were using, rather than prompting them to suggest new specific approaches with the children they had been studying (Edgerton 1994; Plahl 2000). Warwick, on the other hand, was testing out new ways of working by including parents in the sessions and working in the children's homes, neither of which she had done before. Warwick concluded that working in this way was beneficial to families and children, but she conceded that there were limitations for music therapists working in the clients' homes, such as lack of equipment and privacy (Warwick 1995).

In a recent PhD research project, Holck (2004) analysed in detail how different music therapists established contact with six children, some of whom had ASD. She found that, in the basic forms of non-verbal communication between the therapist and the child, an interaction theme specific to each child is built up around a core motive and is then repeated and varied. Holck's description of her work seems similar to the way I would describe my initial process of establishing contact with children with ASD. Like Holck, I feel that this basic non-verbal interaction is very similar to mother–baby interactions.

The literature review indicated that, although there is a wide range of articles describing successful music therapy case studies and a number of articles outlining particular music therapy approaches in this field, there are relatively few experimental research investigations. Those that have been reported indicate that music therapy seems to be effective with children with ASD but that further research would be useful. Although there are some common points and overlaps between my research and previous projects, my study does not duplicate other work and is sufficiently different from previous research to be worthwhile.

Main research hypotheses

- Progress towards achieving identified aims for each of the children could be identified over a period of 18 to 26 weeks.

- Across the ten children, it would become clear that music therapy was effective at achieving some aims, and less effective at achieving others.

- Patterns showing how progress is achieved over time will become clear.

- Parents' patterns of interactions with their children, or perceptions of their children, may change during the course of treatment.

To maintain confidentiality I have used the children's first initial (and sometimes first two initials) and have always referred to the parents as individual children's 'mother' or 'father'.

Methodology

Ten pre-school children on the autistic spectrum who were referred to me for music therapy treatment at the CDC were investigated. This number was chosen because it was a realistic number of children to investigate within the two-year time span allocated for experimental work, and also because by studying ten children I was able to compare how different children with similar difficulties progressed and to evaluate what particular aims music therapy was effective at achieving.

Each child received 18 to 26 weekly individual music therapy sessions (corresponding to two school terms) with their parent or carer in the room. Each of the sessions was videotaped, and the videos were subjected to analysis. The parents were also interviewed before and after treatment and completed a detailed questionnaire to determine how they felt their child was functioning as well as to establish whether their perception of their child had changed during the treatment.

While most children with ASD seem to benefit from music therapy, early intervention may be the most effective time to set up healthy patterns of communication. These patterns need to be explored and shared with parents who will naturally be in attendance with very young children. The parents themselves also often particularly benefit from support and encouragement at this time. From my clinical experience it appears that, at this age, two terms is usually enough time to enable changes to occur, which will, it is hoped, then help the child into nursery, primary school or special education.

In this project I decided to focus purely on the music therapy sessions rather than attempting to compare them with another therapeutic approach. This was partly because of the difficulty involved in matching pre-school ASD children with an appropriate control group, and also because of the difficulty of finding any on-going individual therapy that these children might be involved in on a weekly basis for comparison. Although the lack of a control group means that my results are weakened (as progress in the children could be attributed to maturation), my main focus in this study was to find out more about my work rather than to try to prove that music therapy was effective. One of the strengths of this design was that I was able to look at which particular aims were being met for individual children because it was possible to compare progress on different aims. In addition, as I was studying ten children and their parents, I was able to look at which aims music therapy was particularly successful at achieving, across the ten children.

The research design I used here was a series of 'single-subject experimental designs' (Kazdin 1982; Morley and Adams 1989). However, I did not use a traditional single-case design whereby baseline observations are made, treatment is applied and then changes are evaluated; the original single-case design model was designed for clinical interventions where sudden marked changes occur (Kazdin 1982). In my work with pre-school children with ASD, I was not expecting sudden marked changes but was hoping for gradual slow and progressive changes, so I gathered information by making many repeated measurements of each session. It could be argued that the research design would have been strengthened by adding a baseline period. Nevertheless it is not clear what activities it would have been appropriate to use for all ten children across the baseline period.

All the sessions were videotaped and then analysed by the research assistant, using a five-second sampling system developed in my previous research projects. Five-second samples were used because some of the children responded only in small ways and it was felt that if longer time samples had been used important responses might have been missed. In fact the analysis showed that many of the recorded behaviours occurred across consecutive five-second intervals, indicating that this interval was short enough to capture important aspects of the children's behaviour.

The research assistant did not start analysing videotapes until treatment on a particular child was complete, and she did not feed back her results to me until all the experimental work had been completed. These detailed observations of every single session meant that I could get an objective view of what was occurring in the music therapy sessions, as well as evaluating the parents' feedback, which occurred after every session.

In addition the parents were interviewed, and they completed questionnaires before and after the treatment, providing us with additional data to supplement the information obtained from the video analyses.

Over a period of 26 months, ten pre-school children (under four) with ASD who were referred to music therapy at the CDC were included in the investigation. Some of the children had learning difficulties and others did not, but all were diagnosed as having ASD. None of them had received music therapy treatment before the project started.

After the first two music therapy assessment sessions, which aimed to determine that the child would benefit from further music therapy, I invited the mother (or primary carer) to participate in the study. I explained the project, gave her an information sheet, and asked her to sign a consent form. At any one time I was treating three or four of the ten children.

Setting the aims

After the two music therapy assessment sessions, I discussed with each parent what they felt the particular needs of their child were. Together, we then determined objectives for each of the children. These aims were based on:

- the parent's knowledge of the child
- the results of the two music therapy assessment sessions
- my previous experience of children with similar strengths and difficulties
- the initial music therapy referral letter.

Some aims were shared amongst many children, whereas others were more specific to individual children. 'Increase interactions/exchanges/dialogues', for example, was an aim for all the children except for one who was a year younger than the others and very withdrawn and isolated. The aim for him was simply to 'increase any communicative efforts' on his part.

Some of the aims were linked to the children's levels of ability. Two of the children who were already using words when treatment began did not need to be encouraged to vocalise or use words. Other aims such as 'increase tolerance of direction' or 'discourage child from drawing adults into conflicts with the child' were associated with particular areas of difficulty that some of the children were experiencing.

It is interesting, but not surprising given the nature of autism, that most of the aims were connected with helping the children to communicate.

Videotaping the sessions

The music therapy research assistant videoed almost all the sessions and the verbal reviews that I had with the parents after every session.

Although the children were aware of the camera, I do not think they were in any way inhibited by it. The research assistant would sometimes change position and the children would look up at her, but she was quiet and unobtrusive and I never felt that the camera was a major distraction.

Some of the parents were a little inhibited by the camera at first, but when we talked openly about this and I attempted to reassure the parents, the initial unease was usually quickly dispelled.

Video analysis

Once treatment with a particular child was over, the research assistant was able to start analysing the videotapes of that particular child. She analysed the videos in random order, so that her possible expectations of progress would not influence her results. She analysed a total of 222 videos, which took her around 200 hours. Given the large numbers of videos and the huge amount of time spent analysing them, it is unlikely that she would have remembered details of sessions she had previously videoed sufficiently well to allow her possible expectations of progress to influence her results.

The video analysis system she used was the one that had been developed for my two previous music therapy research projects (Oldfield and Adams 1990; Oldfield, Bunce and Adams 2003).

For each of the children, the treatment objectives were translated into observable behaviours that could be counted and timed. These codes were then marked down in a time grid where every square represented five seconds. Important behaviours by the parents as well as by myself were also coded in a separate row of five-second time grids. As the treatment objectives varied for each parent and child dyad, the codes used for each were different. Before starting analyses on a new child the research assistant would meet with me to determine exactly what she should be looking out for and work out which codes she should use.

I was aware that with only one camera some aims such as 'increasing eye-contact' would not be possible to measure in a reliable way. Similarly, it was not possible to gauge the child's eye direction towards myself or the parent as we all moved around and all three people were not always in the picture. However, I felt that there were enough behaviours that we could measure to be able to get some idea of how the child and the parent were progressing in the sessions.

Table 7.1 shows all the codes used across the ten children and which codes were used for each child.

Table 7.1 Video analysis codes for the ten children

Codes	Children for whom codes were used									
e (Engaged)	W	J	Mi	I	Ma	E	R	M	H	B
ex (Engaged with instrument/choosing)	W	J	Mi	I	Ma	E	R	M	H	
i (Initiating)						E				B
m (Active music making)	W	J	Mi	I	Ma	E	R	M	H	B
mx (Playing with help)		J	Mi				R	M	H	
v (Vocalising spontaneously)	W	J	Mi	I	Ma	E	R	M	H	B
w (Using words)	W			I	Ma					
ts (Talks spontaneously)						E				B
mo (Moves playfully)	W	J	Mi	I	Ma	E	R	M	H	B
s (Sings song)	W						R	M		
sm (Smiles)									H	

Codes	W	J	Mi	I	Ma	E	R	M	H	B
r (Rejects/resists)				I	Ma	E			H	
n (Negative behaviour)	W	J	Mi	I	Ma	E	R	M	H	B
c (Crying)			Mi							
ve (Vocalises echolalically)										B
te (Talks echolalically)						E				B
t (Goes to toilet)										B
im (Interacts with mother)	W	J	Mi	I		E	R	M	H	B
id (Interacts with father)					Ma					B
ra (Responds to music therapist)					Ma	E				B
rm (Responds to mother)						E				B
rd (Responds to father)					Ma					B
pc (Physical contact with mother)								M		
os (Out of shot)	W	J	Mi	I	Ma	E	R	M	H	B
b (Blank)	W	J	Mi	I	Ma	E	R	M	H	B
av (A vocalises)	W	J	Mi	I	Ma	E	R	M	H	B
ao (A plays other instruments)	W	J	Mi	I	Ma	E	R	M	H	B
ap (A plays piano)	W	J	Mi	I	Ma	E	R	M	H	B
ac (A plays clarinet)	W	J	Mi	I	Ma	E	R	M	H	B
as (A sings song)	W	J	Mi	I	Ma	E	R	M	H	B
apl (A moves playfully)	W	J	Mi	I	Ma	E	R	M	H	B
ae (A attempts to engage)	W	J	Mi	I	Ma	E	R	M	H	B
af (A follows)	W	J	Mi	I	Ma	E	R	M	H	B
ab (A blank or out of shot)	W	J	Mi	I	Ma	E	R	M	H	B

Codes	Children for whom codes were used									
mi (Mother attempts to engage/initiates)	W	J	Mi	I		E	R	M	H	B
mp (Mother plays)	W		Mi	I	Ma	E	R	M	H	B
ms (Mother sings)	W								H	
mf (Mother follows)			Mi	I		E				B
mt (Mother talks)						E				
mpl (Mother moves playfully)				I						
di (Father attempts to engage/initiates)					Ma				H	B
dp (Father plays)					Ma				H	B
df (Father follows)					Ma					B
ds (Father sings)									H	
dt (Father talks)					Ma					
tb (Total boxes)	W	J	Mi	I	Ma	E	R	M	H	B

Most of the children's codes are self-explanatory. However, 'engaged' (e) or 'negative' (n) need to be defined. 'Engaged' meant that the child was in some way being communicative, looking up or gesturing *to* the music therapist. For three of the children (Ma, E and B), I made a distinction between 'engaged' and 'responding to music therapist' because I was particularly interested in these children's spontaneous communication as well as the responses to my attempts to communicate with them. For the other children any communicative attempt with me came under the category 'engaged'.

'Negative' behaviours were when a child clearly rebelled, pushed something away or screamed in a cross way, but not when a child withdrew quietly. When the research assistant was in any doubt about interpreting a behaviour, she did not score.

The fact that these behaviours were grouped together and coded as 'negative' did not mean that the process of being angry was considered as being undesirable. It is recognised that expressing anger may well be part of the therapeutic process. I felt that it would be useful to see how frequent these particular behaviours were and when they occurred.

This table shows that while some codes – particularly those relating to the music therapist – were similar across all the children, many other codes were used only for some of the children depending on what the specific aims for each child were. For those children with large amounts of codes, such as B and E, the research assistant usually had to view the videos several times in order to collect all the necessary information.

To help her to keep track of time as she watched the videos, the research assistant used an electronic metronome set at five beats to the bar, where a beat occurred every second. On every fifth beat a bell would sound indicating that she needed to move on to the next grid. The use of the metronome to help with video analysis was developed by Bunce in my previous music therapy project with mothers and young children and had previously been a reliable and accurate way to gather data (Oldfield *et al.* 2003). The video analysis started at the same time for every child, on the 'lo' part of the first 'hello' in the music therapist's greeting song. An excerpt of a completed video analysis form is included as Appendix 10.

After the research assistant had analysed around 15 videotapes, the research consultant checked three different videotapes chosen at random to confirm agreement on the consistent use of the codes. Later, after all the videotapes had been analysed, he randomly analysed another two videotapes and found that he still agreed with her results, indicating that her analyses had been reliable. In the light of the experience gained using these methods in two previous investigations (Oldfield and Adams 1990; Oldfield *et al.* 2003), and also because of lack of time, it was not felt necessary to check inter-observer reliability in a more formal way.

The video analysis system developed by Plahl (2000), which she has called 'Kamuthe', has some similarities with the system I use here. However, her very detailed coding system is the same for all the children she analyses and is not tailored to the individual aims of the children. In her research project, she analyses only the first and the last five minutes of every thirty-minute session. It is interesting to note that even though Plahl was able to use a computer program to help with the video analyses, she still found that each minute she analysed took 30 minutes to complete. Although the research assistant did have to take additional time at the start of analysis on each new child to practise using the new codes, she then found that she could analyse each half-hour tape in one to one-and-a-half hours.

Burford (1988) used video analyses to look at repetitive movements of children with profound learning disabilities and their carers. Recordings were made via a two-camera system. The videos were analysed using an electronic time counter inserted on the screen to record real time to 1/100 second and frame-by-frame analysis. Unfortunately, this system would not have been viable for our analyses as we were trying to observe many different behaviours both for individual children and across the ten different experimental subjects. It was also unnecessary for us to time the behaviours we were analysing as accurately as in Burford's study.

Interpreting the video analysis data

Once the research assistant had analysed all the videotapes, she and I counted all the codes for the children and the parents. This counting was very time-consuming and took around half an hour per video. This meant that a total of around 110 hours was spent counting codes. These figures were then converted to percentages of total time codes recorded in each session in order to take account of the fact that each session varied in length. The percentages were subjected to statistical analysis. In addition to descriptive statistics showing means and highest and lowest scores, I used Kendall's non-parametric correlation test. This test is recommended as being appropriate for this type of data by Morley and Adams (1991). It explores whether there is a trend over time (increase or decrease across sessions) in the behavioural scores. I typed all the figures into the Statistical Package for Social Sciences (SPSS version 11.0) computer program and was then able to subject the data to statistical analysis.

Graphs and pie charts were then used to illustrate the results. I used graphs to show the changes in the children and the parents' behaviours over time. The pie charts were used to illustrate how I used my time in the sessions. When looking at my own behaviours I was more interested in how much time I spent playing different instruments than the patterns of my playing habits over time.

In addition to counting up total numbers of each of the codes, I also counted up the length of some of the children's playing bouts in order to find out whether the amount of time children could focus on any one activity increased or decreased. I looked at the mean length of the playing bouts and the longest playing bouts for each of the sessions.

For the children and the parents I focused on how each of the behaviours we counted changed over time, because one of my hypotheses had been that I would be able to see such changes. When looking at the data on my behaviour in the sessions, I looked at mean percentages in order to get an idea of how I distributed my time and how this varied across the ten children.

When I first set up this investigation, I had also hoped to be able to look in detail at how what I did as a music therapist in the session affected the child's responses. Unfortunately, because of the huge amount of data we had to analyse, I did not have time to do this. This meant that some aims such as 'increasing turn taking' or 'encouraging imitation' could not be evaluated specifically in this investigation.

Structured interviews

The aims of the two structured interviews were to determine how the parents perceived their children and what the parents thought about music therapy. The research assistant conducted all the semi-structured interviews and it was explained to the parents that I would not have access to this information until after their treatment had ended. This was to try to ensure that the parents did not feel (consciously or unconsciously) that they had to say the right things to ensure that their child received good treatment.

In the initial interview, I wanted to find out:

- what the parent hoped music therapy would achieve for the child
- what the parent felt the child would get out of the sessions
- what the parent hoped to get out of the sessions himself or herself.

This initial interviewing was conducted after each family had had two music therapy assessment sessions and it had been agreed that they would benefit from music therapy treatment. This meant that the parents had already seen their child in music therapy assessment sessions and could have some idea of what to expect in the future.

In the interviews after the treatment, I wanted to know whether the parents' views about their children had changed in any way, their general views of the music therapy treatment, and what progress they felt their children had made. The main areas covered were:

- generally inviting the parent to comment on how the music therapy sessions had progressed and what her or his impressions were

- whether the parent's initial expectations had been met (if appropriate, the research assistant would remind the parent of what she or he had said in the initial semi-structured interview).

The research assistant took notes after every semi-structured interview and each of the interviews was also audiotaped.

Some of the questions asked are similar to those asked in Plahl's semi-structured interview (Plahl 2000). However, she focused less on how the parent's perception of the child might have changed and did not have individual treatment objectives for each child.

Parenting Stress Index (PSI) forms

The PSI is a psychological multiple-choice test developed by R. Abidin, in the USA, over a period of 25 years (Abidin 1995). It looks at levels of stress parents are experiencing by asking questions relating to how they are experiencing their own children and how they feel themselves. The two sets of questions are grouped in 'child domain' questions and 'parent domain' questions, and figures from the two areas are then added together to give an indication of the 'total stress' experienced by the parent. The professional manual that comes with the tests explains very clearly how the results of the questionnaires should be worked out and interpreted.

When she conducted the semi-structured interviews before and after treatment, the music therapy research assistant explained about the PSI and gave the parents the questionnaires to fill in at home.

Results of the study

In this study, I was able to gather different types of data on each child and parent. I will now consider the results across the ten families, looking at:

- the music therapy reports
- the video analysis
- the parents' semi-structured interviews and PSIs.

The music therapy reports

I have drawn out a few salient points from each report to give an impression of the progress made by each of the families. These reports are based on my opinions and impressions. This is why I refer to how I felt the children were progressing, in contrast to the results from the video analysis where the data was less subjective.

- W's report indicated that he made good progress during his music therapy sessions. His communication skills particularly seemed to have improved. However, I did remark that his behaviour was often unpredictable and very dependent on the mood he was in on any particular occasion. Although he missed his mother when she was not there, he did not seem too distressed that she was not present for quite a number of his sessions. His mother enjoyed playing and singing with him when she was able to be present.

- J showed an interest in musical exchanges with me right from the beginning. Much of the work we did was to intensify our communication and to improve the quality of our exchanges. In general, I thought that he made good progress. He continued to thoroughly enjoy communicating with both me and his mother through playful sound exchanges. I felt that his vocalisations and words had increased and that his concentration had improved.

- Mi was over a year younger than the other children in this project. He was very isolated and my aims were to draw him out of his isolation and help him to be involved in some playing or communicating with me or his mother. I felt he made progress in these areas and was particularly pleased that he and his mother were able to enjoy some basic interactive music making in the sessions.

- I's report indicated that she made progress in most areas during her music therapy sessions. Although she still struggled to accept direction, she gradually was able to conform to the structure of the session. She was creative and inventive and many interactive musical games involving 'I', her mother and myself evolved. As sessions progressed, she seemed to become more communicative and playful, using more words and pretend play.

- Both Ma and his father were very active in the music therapy sessions and enjoyed playing anything on offer for long periods of time. As sessions progressed, Ma became slightly less lost in his own playing. I felt that his communication gradually became more spontaneous and that his vocalisations and words increased. Ma's father was often involved with Ma, usually playing simultaneously with his son. As the weeks went by he seemed to take a little more of a supportive role, not playing quite so much and listening more to Ma.

- E's report made it clear that a lot of the work with E focused on increasing E's tolerance of adult direction and helping his musical interactions and his communication generally to be less rigid and more spontaneous. He particularly enjoyed playful musical exchanges with his mother and me, which involved drama and changes of leadership. In general the report indicated that E made good progress, although he went through a rebellious phase for four weeks shortly after the work began.

- R's report was positive and indicated that he made considerable progress during music therapy sessions. I commented that the work was 'child-centred' and that I often had to follow what R did as he wandered around the room, in order to get his attention.

- For M, I reported that he had very intense and sometimes emotional reactions in the music therapy sessions. He could become very engaged and involved, but his behaviour was unpredictable and his moods would often quickly fluctuate from one extreme to the other.

- H's report indicated that he enjoyed the music therapy sessions, sometimes losing himself in his playing. His levels of engagement seemed to vary from week to week, but I felt that music therapy was a good way to gain his attention and interest.

- B's report showed that, although he was shy and tentative at first, he gradually came out of himself and became more and more playful, spontaneous and interactive. His concentration improved and he used more and more vocalisations and then words.

All these music therapy reports were positive, indicating either that the children and the parents clearly enjoyed music making or that real progress had been achieved. With all the children I felt that some, if not all, of my original aims had been partly or completely achieved. I thought that all the parents were supportive of their children in the sessions.

For some children I recommended further individual music therapy sessions, if possible at the school they were about to start attending. For others, I suggested that they might be ready for group music therapy sessions. For a few, I felt that any type of music group for young children or even music lessons (when they were a little older) might be beneficial.

It would appear from these ten reports that my music therapy approach was generally successful. This is a particularly positive outcome as the ten families were referred in a routine way and were not especially recruited for the research, and were therefore representative of my general caseload.

The video analysis

Table 7.2 shows the significant changes in behaviour across the ten dyads. Considering that all the children were on the autistic spectrum and that the treatment period was only two terms long, it was good that there were so many significant changes in the behaviour over that period. I will now comment on a few of these changes.

CHILDREN'S LEVELS OF ENGAGEMENT AND AMOUNT OF PLAYING OF INSTRUMENTS

The first line in Table 7.2 (e or eadj) shows that four out of the ten children became significantly more engaged as music therapy sessions progressed. The other six children remained stable, and none of the ten children became less engaged as sessions evolved. The third line, on the other hand, shows that four of the children's amount of active playing significantly decreased as music therapy sessions progressed. Only one child's playing significantly increased and one child's longest playing bouts increased. Music therapy therefore enabled four out of the ten children to become significantly more engaged as sessions progressed. As the children became more involved they often actually played less, but perhaps the playing they did do was more communicative.

Figure 7.1 shows W's and B's levels of engagement and amount of playing across the ten sessions. For these two children the pattern of 'engagement' went up while the amount of 'playing' diminished.

Table 7.2 Statistical significance of behaviour changes

Codes (% of interaction)	Children									
	W	J	Mi	I	Ma	E	R	M	H	B
e (or eadj*) (Engaged)	S+	ns	S+	ns	ns	ns	S+	ns	ns	S+
ex (Engaged with instrument/choosing)	ns	ns	ns	ns	ns	ns	ns	ns	ns	
m (Active music making)	S–	ns	ns	S–	S+	ns	ns	S–	ns	S–
mx (Playing with help)		ns	S+			ns		ns		
i (Initiating)						ns				S+
pmo (Moves playfully)	ns	S–	ns	ns	ns	ns	ns	S–		S+
sm (Smiles)								ns		
pc (Physical contact with mother)							S+			
ve (Vocalises echolalically)										S–
v (Vocalises spontaneously)	ns	ns	ns	ns	ns		ns		ns	S+
te (Talks echolalically)						S–				S–
ti (Talks spontaneously)						S+				S+
w (Using words)	ns		S+	ns						
n (Negative behaviour)	ns	ns	S+	ns			S+	S+		
r (Rejects/resists)				ns	ns	ns			ns	
c (Crying)			ns							
ra (Responds to music therapist)					S+	ns				S–
rm or rd (Responds to mother or father)					ns	ns				S–

Codes (% of interaction)	Children									
	W	J	Mi	I	Ma	E	R	M	H	B
im, imadj or id (Interacts with mother or father)	ns	ns	S+	S+	ns	ns	ns	S−	ns	ns
b (Blank)	ns	ns	ns	ns	ns	ns	S+	ns	ns	ns
mp or dp (Mother or father plays)	S+			ns	S−	ns	S−	ns	ns	ns
mi or di (Mother or father attempts to engage/initiates)	S+	ns	S+	ns	ns	S−	S−	ns	S+	S+
mf or df (Mother of father follows)			ns	ns	ns	ns				ns
ms (Mother signs)	S+								S+	
mt (Mother talks)						ns				
mpl (Mother moves playfully)				S+						
Av. L. bouts**		ns	ns	ns			ns	S−	ns	
Longest bouts		ns	ns	ns			ns	S−	S+	

KEY: S+: significant increase; S−: significant decrease; ns: not statistically significant; Blank: not relevant to that child

* In two cases (eadj and imadj for Mi), the figures included one score that was very atypical. Additional significance tests were carried out on the adjusted (adj) figures excluding these atypical scores.

** In addition to counting the number of codes occurring in sessions, for some children I also looked at how long children played for. To do this I worked out how long the average bout of playing instruments was for each session (a bout was defined as two or more consecutive five-second samples where playing occurred). I also recorded some children's longest bout of playing in each session.

Table 7.2 also shows that only two of the children's playing bouts changed significantly. M's average length of bouts and longest bouts significantly decreased, which is not surprising as his overall levels of playing also decreased significantly.

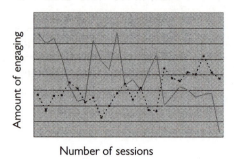

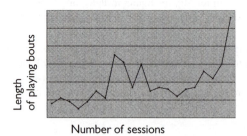

Figure 7.1 W's (top) and B's (bottom) levels of engagement (dotted lines) and amount of playing (continuous lines)

However, it was interesting to find that the length of H's longest bouts in each session significantly increased, as his overall levels of playing did not significantly change. The gradual increase in the length of H's longest playing bouts is illustrated in Figure 7.2.

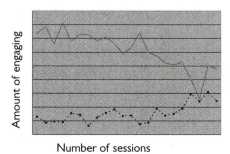

Figure 7.2 H's longest bouts of playing

CHANGES IN VOCALISATIONS OR WORDS

Line 10 (v) in Table 7.2 indicates that, apart from for B, music therapy was not very successful at increasing the children's amount of playful movement or their vocalisations. Perhaps this was because the music therapist used the children's vocalisations as a way to engage the children rather than actively encouraging them to vocalise more. It could also be argued that the children do not vocalise so much during sessions because so many other things are happening and because I am very active myself. However, I do not feel that the children would remain so engaged if the sessions included long periods of inactivity on my part. In addition, parents often report that the children seem to vocalise more *outside* music therapy sessions as a result of the work, even if they do not vocalise so much during the sessions themselves. This was the case for W, J and H.

With the two children (E and B) where an effort was being made to reduce echolalic speech and increase spontaneous speech, both significantly decreased their echolalic speech and increased their spontaneous speech. In addition, B's echolalic vocalisations decreased significantly and his spontaneous vocalisations increased significantly. These results are illustrated in Figure 7.3.

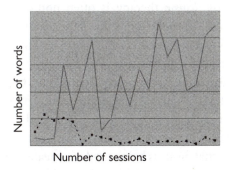

Number of sessions

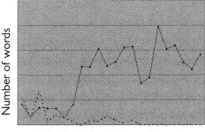

Number of sessions

Figure 7.3 E's (top) and B's (bottom) echolalic speech (dotted lines) and spontaneous speech (continuous lines)

Figure 7.3 shows that music therapy seems to have been effective at decreasing echolalic speech. Together with Figure 7.4, they show also that it was effective at encouraging spontaneous speech.

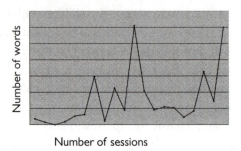

Number of sessions

Figure 7.4 I's use of words

CHANGES IN NEGATIVE BEHAVIOURS

Table 7.2 shows that, for the three behaviours where a decrease might have seemed a positive outcome (n, r and c), none of the children showed any decreases in these areas, and for three children the negative behaviours increased significantly. Music therapy is often non-directive, and as the children become at ease in the sessions it is important that they feel free to express feelings of anger and frustration. Figure 7.5 illustrates the negative behaviours that increased significantly.

These charts show that the three children whose negative behaviours increased significantly (I, R and M) all had initial honeymoon periods where they showed little or no negative behaviours. The child needs time to adapt to a very new situation and to become familiar with both the musical instruments and to the fact that music is being used as a means of interacting. Time is also needed for a trusting relationship to be established between the child and the therapist. Only after the child feels at ease will he or she feel safe to display challenging behaviour. Nordoff and Robbins (1977) were aware in their rating scales of the positive aspects of some children's resistance, noting that levels of resistance were found to increase as participation also increased.

In addition, it is important that, in spite of an escalation of difficult behaviours, none of the children's levels of engagement decreased signifi-

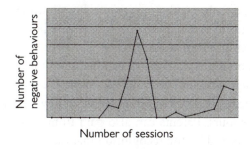

Number of sessions

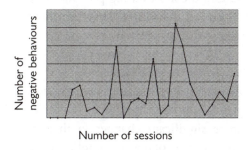

Number of sessions

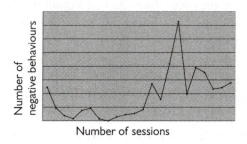

Number of sessions

Figure 7.5 I's (top), R's (middle) and M's (bottom) negative behaviours

cantly. For some children it is important to know that they can express rebellious feelings that can be heard and understood. The act of expressing strong emotions can relieve tension and could in some cases cut down on negative behaviours outside the music therapy sessions. Thus, in some situations the fact that a child's negative behaviours increase in music therapy sessions could be an indication that the child is in a constructive therapeutic process. For some parents (this is shown later in this chapter for M's mother), the fact that the child can openly express negative feelings outside the home which are contained within a therapeutic situation can be a great relief and diminish their own levels of stress.

It is also important to note that it can be useful for parents if children show some of their difficult behaviours in music therapy sessions, as they might then be able to get new ideas from me about how to deal with or think about these behaviours. Parents can also gain from 'sharing' their child's difficult behaviours and by the recognition that looking after their child is often hard work. Perhaps it is not a coincidence that the two mothers whose PSI stress levels reduced the most during pre- and post-treatment were R's and M's mothers. Both R's and M's negative behaviours increased significantly during the music therapy sessions.

CHANGES IN THE PARENTS' BEHAVIOURS

The parents' significant behaviour changes are shown in lines 21 (mp), 22 (mi), 23 (mf), 24 (ms), 25 (mt) and 26 (mpl) in Table 7.2. Eight out of the ten parents showed some significant changes in their behaviours in music therapy sessions. There were a total of 12 significant changes. Eight of these changes were increases and four were decreases. Four out of the ten parents' levels of engagement (mi) with their children significantly increased during music therapy treatment. It was interesting to see that the two parents who seemed to want to sing with their children were able to do so significantly more as the music therapy sessions progressed. These findings suggest that music therapy seems to have been successful in involving parents in the work and helping them to enjoy engaging with their children.

It must also be added that, for Ma and E, the fact that the parents played less and attempted to engage less was actually a positive change as they both gained from taking more time to sit back and listen to their child. Ma's father in particular identified this as one of the important things he had learnt from music therapy sessions. R's mother, whose playing and attempting to engage also significantly reduced, explained to us that she had made a choice to intervene less as she felt this allowed R to be more easily involved with me and she wanted to enjoy observing him interacting with me. Later I show that her stress levels were reduced pre- and post-treatment, so she also gained from music therapy treatment even though her active participation did not increase.

WAYS IN WHICH MY TIME WAS DISTRIBUTED DURING THE SESSIONS

The pie charts in Figure 7.6 illustrate the mean percentage of my activities in sessions across the ten children. The total of these percentages adds up to more than 100 because a lot of the time I was playing, singing and moving simultaneously. These pie charts show that I spent more time vocalising with the children than on anything else. Although I was aware that I spent a lot of time in this way, I had no idea how high this percentage was. Figure 7.6 shows that I spent 88 per cent of my time being 'active'.

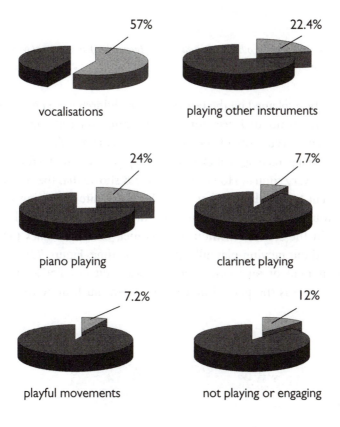

Figure 7.6 Mean percentages of Amelia's activities in music therapy sessions across the ten children

Figure 7.7 shows how – with quite a number of the children – when the piano playing was high, the other instrument playing was low (and vice versa).

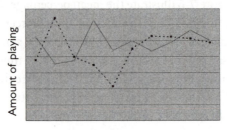

Figure 7.7 A's percentages of other instrument playing (dotted line) and piano playing (continuous line) across the ten children

This could be explained by the fact that when children were not particularly drawn to the piano, or I was not able to capture their attention from the piano, I then played more of the other instruments myself.

My overall percentages of clarinet playing (7.7%) and playful movement (7.2%) were very similar. However, Figure 7.8 shows that the two activities do not seem to correlate in any way. This was quite surprising as I often moved around the room while playing the clarinet. Clearly I also moved playfully in the sessions without my clarinet, and sometimes played the clarinet without moving playfully at the same time. Figure 7.8 shows also that the amount of my clarinet playing was quite similar across the ten children, whereas the playful movement varied much more from child to child.

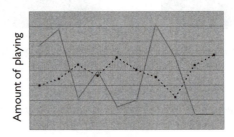

Figure 7.8 A's percentages of clarinet playing (dotted line) and playful movement (continuous line) across the ten children

Parents' semi-structured interviews and PSIs

Information was gathered from the semi-structured interviews carried out by the research assistant with each of the parents before and after treatment. For the pre-treatment interview I consulted her written notes on the forms used to guide the interview. For the post-treatment interview I listened to the audiotape of the interview and made notes as I listened.

In summary, nine out of the ten parents were very positive about the music therapy treatment. The only one who was not completely positive was Mi's mother. She said that music therapy worked but was very cross with me for stopping the sessions, which she felt were the one thing that her son had responded to. So, in a sense, this was also positive.

Many of the parents were very insightful about the processes involved in the treatment and felt that they, as well as the children, had gained confidence and new ideas.

Table 7.3 shows the PSI results across the ten parents. All the figures in the child domain are very high except for M's mother's post-treatment figures. This is understandable as all the children had a diagnosis of autism and it would be surprising if parents were not concerned about the children's difficulties.

The parent domain figures vary much more, indicating that parents' general circumstances and general levels of stress are very different from one another.

Most of the parents' overall levels of stress vary very little post-treatment. However, R's and M's mothers' levels of stress were considerably reduced post-treatment.

Review of main findings and conclusions

One of the interesting things about this research investigation was that I studied ten children and their parents in depth, using four ways of gathering information: music therapy reports, video analysis, semi-structured parent interviews and the PSI questionnaires for parents. I obtained different information from these methods of collecting data, which gave me a very complete picture of each of the dyads.

The music therapy reports were generally positive, indicating that I felt the therapy had been useful and that the children and the parents had responded well. The video analysis showed some positive changes for each of the ten dyads. Considering that all the children were on the autistic

Table 7.3 PSI results for the ten parents

	Total child domain (centiles)		Total parent domain (centiles)		Total stress (centiles)	
	Pre-treatment	Post-treatment	Pre-treatment	Post-treatment	Pre-treatment	Post-treatment
W's mother	91	97	70	68	82	88
J's mother	96	98	50	39	81	81
Mi's mother	99+	99+	72	85	98	99+
I's mother	97	98	82	80	93	93
Ma's father	99+	92	6	*	62	*
E's mother	99+	99+	82	79	97	94
R's mother	99+	91	93	72	98	85
M's mother	99+	76	49	30	90	50
H's mother	97	99+	97	96	98	99+
B's mother	93	90	24	23	63	61

* Ma's father did not fill in the questionnaire for these sections.

spectrum, and that the period of intervention was relatively short (18–26 weekly sessions), this was a very positive result. However, the music therapy reports tended to be more positive than the video analysis data. M, for example, did not show many significant improvements in the video analysis, although the music report was generally positive. There could be several explanations for the differences in these data.

- First, the video analysis and the way I have analysed the data does not show subtle changes in the *quality* of communication between the child and the parent, or between the child and myself. I was not able to measure increases in eye-contact or turn-taking skills, for example.

- Second, some children's negative behaviours may increase in music therapy sessions without this necessarily being a sign of deterioration. If children are feeling cross or rebellious it is a positive sign that they can express these feelings within the music therapy sessions. Parents can benefit from seeing another adult dealing with these behaviours and may gain ideas for new management strategies.

- Third, my music therapy report will deliberately focus on positive aspects of the child's and the parent's behaviour as this is part of my general approach. This does not mean that I ignore or under-estimate the difficulties families are experiencing, but rather that I try to help to put these difficulties in perspective and remind the families of the things that *are* working.

The video analysis also showed that, for a number of the children, as their levels of engagement increased, the amount they actually played the instruments decreased. Although this makes sense, it was not a result I had expected. It was also very exciting to find from the semi-structured interviews that all the parents felt positive about the music therapy treatment. The video analysis confirmed this finding, as some aspects of seven out of the ten parents' interactive behaviours changed significantly. Two of the parents whose behaviours did not change were the mothers of M and R, who both chose to take a listening rather than an active role within the sessions. It is interesting to note from the PSI results that these two mothers' stress levels went down considerably post-treatment, indicating that they also benefited.

When looking at the ways in which I distributed my time, I was surprised to find how much I vocalised. It was also interesting to find that, overall, I spent roughly the same amount of time playing the piano as other instruments and the same amount of time playing the clarinet as moving playfully. Nevertheless, the proportions varied for each dyad. Having looked in such detail at this material, it may now be possible to use the pie charts as a norm or a characteristic way in which I distribute my time in sessions.

Thinking back to my main research hypotheses (see earlier in the chapter), I have clearly been able to confirm the first, second and fourth hypotheses and have learnt a considerable amount about my work in the process. The third hypothesis has not been so clearly demonstrated, apart from the fact that I was able to identify that a number of children went through a honeymoon period before exhibiting negative behaviours in the sessions. Perhaps longer treatment periods would be necessary before patterns of behaviour over time become apparent.

The Music Therapy Charity has agreed to fund a further small post-doctoral investigation to allow me to enter all the video analysis data (and not just total codes and length of bouts as I have done in this investigation) into the computer. A special computer program has been devised to analyse the data in more depth. This work is on-going and will enable me to answer questions relating to how the children's, the parents' and my behaviours affected one another.

Overall, this study has had very positive results, which have enabled me to understand and define my particular approach with this client group. I now have additional confidence to pursue this way of working and to continue to develop my approach as I learn from each new case.

Conclusion

This book began with a description of my general music therapy approach and then four chapters about working with individual pre-school children and their parents at the Child Development Centre (CDC) in Cambridge. Two of these four chapters on my work at the CDC were about children with autistic spectrum disorders, one was about children with severe physical and mental difficulties and one was about children with no clear diagnosis. The following chapter was about group work, and the next was about research with children with autistic spectrum disorder. This primary focus on clinical work indicates that 'interactive music therapy' has evolved first from clinical practice, and then from teaching music therapy students, writing about music therapy and research.

The book started with two vignettes and then went on to include 26 further case studies and short reports on children and families. Some children and parents have been described in detail, others summarised in a short paragraph. In a number of cases parents' and colleagues' reports have been included alongside my accounts. Each case is different and unique and has been included to show different aspects of my work. However, I have also been able to show that there are common characteristics to my approach. With pre-school children with autistic spectrum disorder and their parents I identified eight points that are central to my approach. These are:

- the motivating aspect of music therapy sessions
- the structure inherent in the sessions and in music making
- the balance between following and initiating
- the basic non-verbal exchanges
- the fact that children can be in control in a constructive way
- movement combined with music
- playfulness and drama in the music
- working jointly with parents.

In Chapter 3, I explained that many music therapists have written about work with children with autistic spectrum disorder. The eight points just listed have been mentioned individually in various case studies and theoretical papers. However, a method of working centred around these eight points has not been developed or written about previously.

When looking at how my way of working fitted into other general approaches to children with autistic spectrum disorder, I found that three authors in particular talked about approaches that included the word 'interaction'. Janert (2001) emphasised the importance of interactive games, the speech therapist Prevener (2000) included musical interactive therapy in her work, and Caldwell (2005) developed an approach based on intensive interaction. So here again I find that my approach overlaps with ideas developed by other professionals working with children with autistic spectrum disorder.

With regard to children with severe physical and mental difficulties, I identified nine characteristics that I felt characterised my work, some of which were similar to points in the above list. These are:

- the fact that the therapist may have to initiate rather than follow
- the importance of taking account of physical limitations
- working closely with physiotherapists

- a slower pace of work
- the motivating aspect of music therapy sessions
- developing vocalisations and the use of words
- the fact that children can be in control in a constructive way
- working jointly with parents
- preparing for ending music therapy treatment.

With children with no clear diagnosis, the work will vary more from child to child and will always include aspects from both these lists. However, there are a number of additional issues that are particularly important with this client group. These are:

- the fact that music therapy is very different from other forms of treatment
- the emphasis on focusing on each individual child's and parent's unique strengths and difficulties
- the importance of taking time to gain the child's and the parent's trust
- the importance of focusing on the child's and the parent's strengths
- the fact that difficulties can sometimes be approached indirectly.

With all three of these client groups it is clear that, in the music therapy sessions, the focus is primarily on the interactive process between the therapist and the child, between the child and the parent, and between the therapist and the parent. In other words it is 'interactive music therapy'.

The motivating aspect of music therapy sessions is mentioned in the first two lists, and with the third group the importance of focusing on the child's and the parent's strengths is emphasised. This is why I have called my way of working 'a positive approach'.

I have made it clear that my starting point has been the experience gained from my clinical work. However, I would not have developed this interactive music therapy approach had I not spent time reflecting on my work and then committing thoughts to paper. The first step in this process of reflection has usually been to present case work either to colleagues or to music therapy students. By talking about the clinical processes and inviting discussion, my thoughts have become clearer and I have been able to gain

s. In my book *Interactive Music Therapy in Child and Family Psychia-*
eld 2006), I will explore various aspects of teaching music therapy
ater depth, including running music therapy workshops, teaching
dents and making training videos.

Chapter 7 of the present book is a description of a research investigation
into pre-school children with autistic spectrum disorder and their parents. I
see research investigations such as this as the third step in the process of
developing a specific method or approach, the first step being the clinical
work and the second being the teaching and writing about the work. In this
research investigation many of my ideas about my clinical work were
confirmed. It was encouraging, for example, that many of the children's
levels of engagement increased. It was not surprising to find that I was
actively involved for such a high proportion of the time. It was also gratify-
ing that all the parents felt positive about the work. In many ways this
research confirms the validity of the title I have given to my way of working:
'interactive music therapy, a positive approach'.

Coda

Recently I saw two-year-old Casey and her mother, Eva, for an initial music
therapy assessment session at the CDC. She had already had a diagnosis of
autistic spectrum disorder. Her four-year-old brother, Roger, stayed in the
waiting room with their father. As soon as they walked into the room and
shut the door, Casey started crying loudly. Throughout the session she sat on
her mother's lap sobbing, and at times shaking with distress. Occasionally
she would get up to walk towards the door, only to start crying even more
loudly again when we stopped her from opening the door. On one occasion
she looked at the wind chimes and briefly played with them. When I played
loud music her distress did not escalate; if I stopped playing, however, she
would cry more loudly. Throughout the session, Eva tried to soothe her and
reassure her. She told me that Casey normally loved music but found new situations difficult and particularly disliked being in rooms with the door
closed. I asked Eva whether she would mind trying again and she seemed
happy to come back.

This session was not interactive and certainly not positive. I felt
exhausted after they had left, but knew that I would try again. I thought it
would be important to be clear about the beginning and the end of the
session and to remain positive and warm, giving Casey time to respond in

her own time. I also felt that it would be important to keep reassuring Eva and explaining that I was happy to work through Casey's distress if we both continued to feel that we would eventually be able to help her. The fact that I had an established approach and defined way of working helped me to move forward and think clearly about this case.

The next week, Casey's mother came on her own with the two children. This gave me an opportunity to ignore Casey's crying (which again started as soon as she came in) and to focus entirely on four-year-old Roger who enthusiastically played anything I offered him. After about 15 minutes I noticed that Casey's crying stopped every time I was playing loudly. I kept playing while suggesting to Eva that she could offer Casey the wind chimes. This time Casey played quite definitely, and only resumed her sobbing when the music stopped. Later, I played the ocean drum with Roger on the mat and I noticed Casey looking very curious. Eva gave her an ocean drum to play and she became so absorbed in her playing that she forgot to cry when I stopped playing. Soon after this I went back to the piano and Roger played the drum. This time I was able to offer Casey drumsticks myself and she played very loudly, dancing as she played. She still did not smile or look at me, but we were actively making music together.

After the session Eva and I decided that I would work with Roger and Casey together for the next two weeks, and after half term, when Roger started school full-time, we would continue with Casey and Eva on their own.

My clinical work continues to fascinate and excite me. Each new case brings new challenges. Having a defined and clear approach helps me to meet these challenges. Nevertheless, I am in no doubt that I will continue to learn from each new clinical situation and that my way of working will never stop evolving and developing.

'Hello' song

Music therapy assessment form (stage 1)

Name: **Date:**

Attention, awareness, concentration

Motivation

Communication

Spontaneity, imagination, choice

Any other comments

Suggestions

On-going music therapy assessment form (stage 2)

Up to five therapeutic aims for the sessions should be written into the top row of the form. Each week, the therapist should comment on the progress made towards each of the aims in the boxes below. The form can be used for up to six weeks.

Name: **Time and place of session:**

Date	Aim:	Aim:	Aim:	Aim:	Aim:	Suggestions

Music therapy report form (stage 3)

Name: **DOB:**   **Date:**

Introduction

To include:

- who referred the child or the family
- when the referral was made
- reason for referral (if given)
- history of previous music therapy treatment and/or assessments
- summary of when treatment was given
- frequency, length, individual or group work.

General musical likes and dislikes

General aims or objectives

Progress towards these aims

Parent's role in sessions (if applicable)

Recommendations

Examples of completed report forms can be found on the following pages.

Danny's music therapy report

Name: Danny   **DOB:** DD/MM/YY   **Date:** 3.6.2001

Introduction

Danny was referred to music therapy by the community paediatrician. He was seen at the Child Development Centre for two music therapy assessment sessions with his mother in June 2000, and then had regular weekly, individual music therapy sessions with his mother between October 2000 and May 2001.

General musical likes and dislikes

Although Danny was quite a solitary little boy who often appeared in a world of his own, he consistently showed awareness of music and sounds. He noticed ends of phrases or changes in volume or musical style by looking up or turning around. He often looked up in an expectant way when his vocal sounds or rhythmic stamping were imitated and he would smile happily when an expected event (such as bells falling off our heads) occurred in a familiar song. He clearly recognised some songs and associated certain instruments with expected events (e.g. he quickly realised that the bongo drums were always used as a way of finishing off the session). He was willing to try a variety of musical instruments and particularly liked the ocean drum, the cabassa, the wind chimes, the autoharp, the clarinet and the horn, and latterly the piano and the snare drum. He did not usually use beaters to play the percussion instruments but would occasionally briefly try one tap with a beater before discarding it in favour of his hands. Sometimes he would be interested in feeling the vibrations of an instrument with his hands, his head or his mouth. Having a scarf or a handkerchief around his neck seemed to help divert him from mouthing the instruments, allowing him to use his hands more freely.

General aims or objectives

- To increase the amount of time Danny was willing to be involved in any one activity with me.

- To increase and intensify any communicative efforts by Danny (e.g. eye-contact, imitation or turn-taking).
- To increase Danny's vocalisations and give him a chance to express himself through vocal sounds or other forms of music making.

Progress towards these aims

Although Danny was understandably uneasy at first, he quickly became used to the familiar structure of the sessions and responded very well to the on/off approach which consisted of alternating between me following whatever he was doing and then being a little more directive and guiding him towards a choice of my own. The predictable structure of the session seemed to reassure him, and after a few tears in the first few sessions he was always happy to come into the room. Nevertheless, after 25 minutes to half an hour he would invariably show that he was aware that it was time to bring the session to a close.

Danny usually found it difficult to remain focused on any one activity with me for more than one or two minutes at a time. However, as sessions progressed his ability to concentrate and continue to enjoy a particular instrument with me increased. In the very last session he remained fascinated in playing the snare drum with me for almost five minutes.

The 'safe' predictable structure of the music therapy sessions as well as Danny's obvious interest in sound and music seemed to help him to trust me. In every session, Danny would respond with expectant smiles and clear eye-contact to favourite activities such as 'bells falling off our heads' to the tune of 'London Bridge is Falling Down', and 'the jumping game' where I would play loud chords on the piano while Danny's mother would help him to jump up in the air.

As sessions progressed, he would 'expect' musical responses from both myself and his mother on the clarinet and the horn and sometimes enter into foot stamping exchanges all over the room with me. He also gradually made his intentions clearer to both of us, sometimes pointing or guiding his mother's or my hands to whatever he wanted to play.

Danny's vocalisations would vary from session to session but he did seem to gradually become more vocal, using a wide range of sounds in the first two weeks of May 2001, but then being quieter again in the last two sessions at the end of that same month.

Overall, Danny seemed to make progress in all areas.

Danny's mother's role in these sessions

Danny's mother was always quietly supportive and helpful, showing great understanding and insight into her son's strengths and difficulties. As sessions progressed, she gradually became more involved in playing the instruments herself, as Danny made it clear to both of us that this was what he wanted. He would often look up at her expectantly and she would respond in a sensitive way, waiting for him to look at her before giving her musical answer. At other times he would seek reassurance from her by giving her a cuddle or take her hand to guide her towards an instrument he wanted. The bond between the two of them was obviously very strong and warm. Danny's mother was pleased about his progress in music therapy and willing to help in whatever way she could.

Recommendations

Danny seems to be particularly responsive to music therapy and I would recommend that he should continue to have weekly, individual music therapy sessions. Ideally, it would be best if these music therapy sessions could be provided within the school that Danny attends as it would then be easier to make sure that progress achieved in music therapy sessions generalised to the classroom situation.

Leon's music therapy report

Name: Leon   **DOB:** DD/MM/YY   **Date:** 1.5.2001

Introduction

Leon was referred to music therapy by the consultant community paediatrician from the Child Development Centre in March 2000. He was originally seen for two music therapy assessment sessions with his mother in July 2000. From October 2000 to May 2001, he had weekly, half-hour, individual music therapy sessions with his mother at the centre.

General musical likes and dislikes

Leon was a very active and energetic little boy who quickly showed an interest in a variety of sounds and most of the musical instruments. He particularly loved tapping the beaters together and would happily have rhythmic tapping exchanges with me. He also liked moving, dancing and jumping around the room, often accompanying his movements by excited vocalisations. He would enjoy 'peek-a-boo' type games with me while he was moving around and would notice my imitation of his movements as well as picking up and copying some of my movement ideas. Occasionally, he would get distracted by twirling the cymbal or by taking the notes off the glockenspiel, but generally it was possible to re-interest him in shared music-making with me. As the sessions progressed he showed awareness and sensitivity not only to phrase endings but also to changes of tempo and musical style. He would react excitedly when the music became louder and faster, or when there was an expectant silence. He quickly responded to the predictable structure of the sessions and clearly expected the familiar 'Hello' and 'Goodbye' activities.

General aims or objectives

- To intensify our non-verbal exchanges, helping Leon to take turns with me and also pick up some of my ideas or suggestions.

- To increase Leon's eye-contact and to encourage him to vocalise freely and communicatively.
- To help Leon to accept and enjoy direction.
- To increase Leon's concentration and extend the amount of time he is willing to co-operate with us.

Progress towards these aims

As the weeks went by, Leon's non-verbal musical exchanges with me became longer, more varied and more sophisticated. He enjoyed my imitation of his ideas but was also able to pick up and take on my suggestions.

His eye-contact was good and his vocalisations increased. He used a wide range of vowels with varying pitches and intonation, usually to accompany a movement he was making but also when pointing at an instrument he wanted or when filling in gaps in familiar songs. After a couple of months, he would reliably say 'ei ei' for 'byebye' when we played the bongo drums to finish off the session.

Although we communicated best when I entered into the games that he initiated, Leon was also able to become involved in musical activities that I suggested. It took me several months to show him how to blow down the wind instruments to produce a sound. For many weeks I would play the clarinet and hand him a wind instrument which he would rather reluctantly take from me and quickly put down after one or two unsuccessful attempts. However, he let me persuade him to have one or two tries every week. Eventually he did manage to produce a sound and very much enjoyed blowing down the recorder from then onwards. In the last few sessions he had great fun with an activity where his mother and I pretended to be asleep and he would then 'wake us up' with great bursts of delighted laughter. Even when he was reluctant to become involved in playing an instrument that I offered to him, he would consent to try it once or twice before firmly putting it back on the shelf with the other instruments.

Leon usually made it very clear to us what he wanted to play and when he wanted to finish whatever he was doing. At times he could remain focused on a particular activity for five minutes, but often he would bring games to a close after one or two minutes. Once he had decided that he had had enough it was very difficult to re-engage him in that particular game.

Overall, I feel that Leon made very good progress in his music therapy sessions. As his vocalisations increased he started using some words. His concentration improved and he became more willing to take up other people's ideas or suggestions. Above all, he showed how very much he can enjoy communicating with us through playful sound exchanges. He had an infectious sense of fun, which he wanted to share with both myself and his mother.

Leon's mother's role in the sessions

In general, Leon's mother observed him quietly, providing gentle support and encouragement at just the right moments. Leon frequently went to his mum for a reassuring hug, often looking to check that she was still there. At times, she played instruments with us and in later weeks Leon made a point of giving her instruments to join in with and going to get her, so she played with the two of us. He also became used to sitting on her lap to play the piano and always went to get her when he felt it was time for the three of us to sit at the piano.

Recommendations

Leon is clearly very responsive to music and sounds and can become very engaged and communicative in music therapy sessions. I would strongly recommend that he continues to have regular, weekly, music therapy sessions. These sessions should ideally be provided at his school so that progress achieved in music therapy sessions can more easily generalise to the classroom situation. He may soon be ready for a small music therapy group with two or three other children.

Guiding notes for parents writing about music therapy sessions

Questions to think about when writing

None of these questions *needs* to be answered. If they inspire you, fine – but if not don't feel they have to be answered. Everything on this sheet is just intended as a help but don't feel in any way constrained or limited by what I've put down. Feel free to write as much or as little as you want to.

- Perhaps write a paragraph or two about your initial concerns about your son/daughter, the first months/years, daily life with him/her, his/her particular strengths and difficulties, and also what you particularly enjoy about him/her.

- Why did you first think your son/daughter would benefit from music therapy? How do you use music at home?

- What are your first impressions about music therapy? Any particular concerns?

- What did you feel like being in the music therapy sessions with him/her?

- Do you think he/she has benefited from the sessions? If so, how and why?

- What have *you* particularly enjoyed in the music therapy sessions?

- Do you think it's important to be in the room with your son/daughter during the music therapy sessions? Why?

- What do you hope for in the future: if he/she has more music therapy sessions in school? In general?

Two Makaton songs

In these songs, the words that should be signed have been underlined and put in bold.

I Can Sign...

A Bus Trip

NB: This is based on a song entitled 'The Snake and the Goose' (Warren and Spinks 1982).

Three action songs

In these songs, the words that are accompanied by actions have been put in bold and underlined. The songs 'Different Colour Hats' and 'King/Queen of the Bells' are also included in the book *Pied Piper* (Bean and Oldfield 2001).

Clothes Song

Different Colour Hats

King/Queen of the Bells

Excerpt from a completed video analysis form (minutes 16–23 of the session)

Video Analysis Form

Video Tape Number: 3   Date: 08/03/01
Clients: Mi and Mum
Session Number: 15

Minutes	Seconds											
	5	10	15	20	25	30	35	40	45	50	55	60
16 C	e*	e	e	e	e	im	e	e	e	e	e im	e
A		ac	ac/ mi	ac/ mi	ac/ mf	ac/ mf	ac/ mf	ac/ mi	ac/ mf	ac/ mf	ac/ mf	ac/ mf
17 C	e		e	e	e	e		e	e		e	e
A	ac/ mf	ac	ac/ mi	apl	ac	m/f	apl	ac	m/f	apl /mi	ac	ac
18 C	e	e	e	e im	e	e	e	m	e	im	e	m
A	mi	ac	mi	ac	ac	ac	ac	mi	ac	ac/ mf	mi	ac
19 C	m	m	m	m	m	e		m	m	v		e
A	ac		av ao		af apl	apl	apl	apl	apl	apl	apl	av ao
20 C		e	e	e	e		m	m	m	m		m
A	ap	ap av	ap av	av	av	av	ap av	ap	ap	av		a av
21 C	m	e	e		m	m	m	m	m	v		
A	ap av		av	av	ap av	ap av	ap av	ap av	ap av	av	ap av	ap av

Minutes	Seconds											
22 C		im	im	im	im	im			m	m		v
A	ap av	ap av	ap av	ap av	ap av	ap av	ap av	ap av	ap av	ap av	ap av	ap av
23 C	v	im	im v	v				e			e	
A	ap av	ap av	ap	ap av	ap av	av	ap av			ae	ae	ae

* Codes explained in Table 7.1 in Chapter 7.

Row C refers to child's codes.

Row A refers to Amelia's codes (top line) or parents' codes (bottom line).

References

Aasgaard, T. (2005) 'Assisting children with malignant blood disease to create and perform their own songs.' In F. Baker and T. Wigram (eds) *Songwriting: Methods, Techniques and Clinical Applications for Music Therapy Clinicians, Educators and Students.* London: Jessica Kingsley Publishers.

Abidin, R. (1995) *Parenting Stress Index.* Professional Manual for Psychological Assessment Resources Inc, USA.

Agrotou, A. (1988) 'A case study: Lara.' *British Journal of Music Therapy 2*, 1, 17–23.

Alvin, J. and Warwick, A. (1991) *Music Therapy for the Autistic Child.* Oxford: Oxford University Press.

Bailey, S. (2001) 'Negotiating control and facilitating empowerment: individual music therapy with two children with autism.' MA thesis, Anglia Polytechnic University.

Baron-Cohen, S. and Bolton, P. (1993) *Autism: The Facts.* Oxford: Oxford Medical Publications.

Bean, J. (1995) 'Music therapy and the child with cerebral palsy: directive and non-directive interventions.' In T. Wigram, R. West and B. Saperston (eds) *The Art and Science of Music Therapy: A Handbook.* Chur, Switzerland: Harwood Academic Publishers.

Bean, J. and Oldfield, A. (2001) *Pied Piper: Musical Activities to Develop Basic Skills.* London: Jessica Kingsley Publishers.

Benenzon, R.O. (1982) *Music Therapy in Child Psychosis.* Springfield, IL: Charles C. Thomas.

Bergman, P. and Escola, S. (1949) 'Unusual sensitivities in very young children.' *Psychoanalytic Study of the Child 3*, 4, 333–352.

Bettelheim, B. (1967) *The Empty Fortress: Infantile Autism and the Birth of Self.* New York: Free Press.

Birkeback, M. and Winter, U. (1985) 'Musiktherapie mit autistischen Kindern.' *Beschäftigungstherapie und Rehabilitation 2*, 113–118.

Boon, M. (2002) Unpublished music therapy report.

Boxhill, E.H. (1985) *Music Therapy for the Developmentally Disabled.* Rockville, MD: Aspen Publications.

Brown, S. (1994) 'Autism and music therapy: is change possible and why?' *British Journal of Music Therapy 8*, 1, 15–25.

Brown, S. (2002) 'Hello object! I destroyed you!' In L. Bunt and S. Hoskyns (eds) *The Handbook of Music Therapy.* Hove, East Sussex: Brunner–Routledge.

Bryan, A. (1989) 'Autistic group case study.' *British Journal of Music Therapy 3*, 1, 16–21.

Bullowa, M. (1979) 'Research in prelinguistic communication.' In M. Bullowa (ed) *Before Speech: The Beginning of Interpersonal Communication.* Cambridge: Cambridge University Press.

Bunt, L. and Pavlicevic, M. (2001) 'Music and emotion: perspectives from music therapy.' In N. Juslin and J. Sloboda (eds) *Music and Emotion, Theory and Research.* Oxford: Oxford University Press.

Burday, E.M. (1995) 'The effects of signed and spoken words taught with music on sign and speech by children with autism.' *Journal of Music Therapy 32*, 3, 189–202.

Burford, B. (1988) 'Action cycles: rhythmic actions for engagement with children and young adults with profound mental handicap.' *European Journal of Special Needs Education 3*, 4, 189–206.

Caldwell, P. (2005) *Finding You, Finding Me.* London: Jessica Kingsley Publishers.

Carr, A. (1999) *The Handbook of Child and Adolescent Clinical Psychology: A Contextual Approach.* Hove: Brunner–Routledge.

Clark, C. and Donna, C. (1979) *Clinically Adapted Instruments for the Multiply Handicapped: A Source Book.* St Louis, MO: Magnamusic–Baton.

Clarkson, G. (1998) *I Dreamed I was Normal: A Music Therapist's Journey into the Realms of Autism.* St Louis, MO: Magnamusic–Baton.

Coates, S. (2001) 'The relationship IS the thing.' In J. Richer and S. Coates (eds) *Autism: The Search for Coherence.* London: Jessica Kingsley Publishers.

Darnley-Smith, R. and Patey, H. (2003) *Music Therapy.* London: Sage.

Di Franco, G. (1999) 'Music and autism: vocal improvisation as containment of stereotypes.' In T. Wigram and J. De Backer (eds) *Music Therapy in Developmental Disability, Paediatrics and Neurology.* London: Jessica Kingsley Publishers.

Edgerton, C. (1994) 'The effect of improvisational music therapy on the communicative behaviours of autistic children.' *Journal of Music Therapy 31,* 1, 31–62.

Euper, J.A. (1968) 'Early infantile autism.' In E.T. Gaston (ed) *Music in Therapy.* New York: Macmillan.

Evers, S. (1992) 'Early infantile autism.' In E.T. Gaston (ed) *Music in Therapy.* New York: Macmillan.

Frith, U. (1990) *Autism.* Oxford: Basil Blackwell.

Gembris, H. (1995) 'Musikalische Entwicklungspsychologie und ihre mögliche Bedeutung für die Musiktherapie.' *Musiktherapeutische Umschau 16,* 93–107.

Griessmeier, B. (1994) *Musiktherapie mit Krebstkranken Kindern.* Stuttgart: Bärenreiter Verlag.

Gustorff, D. and Neugebauer, L. (1988) 'Ein Lied, ein Lied fur Bahmam.' *Musiktherapeutische Umschau 9,* 79–88.

Heal-Hughes, M. (1995) 'A comparison of mother and infant interactions and the client–therapist relationship in music therapy.' In T.Wigram, B. Saperston and R. West (eds) *The Art and Science of Music Therapy: A Handbook.* Chur, Switzerland: Harwood Academic Publishers.

Holck, U. (2004) 'Turn taking in music therapy with children with communication disorders.' *British Journal of Music Therapy 18,* 2, 45–54.

Howat, R. (1995) 'Elizabeth: a case study of an autistic child in individual music therapy.' In T. Wigram, B. Saperston and R. West (eds) *The Art and Science of Music Therapy: A Handbook.* Chur, Switzerland: Harwood Academic Publishers.

Howlin, P., Baron-Cohen, S. and Hadwin, J. (1999) *Teaching Children with Autism to Mind-read.* New York: John Wiley and Sons.

Janert, S. (2001) 'The young autistic child: reclaiming non-autistic potential through interactive games.' In J. Richer and S. Coates (eds) *Autism: The Search for Coherence.* London: Jessica Kingsley Publishers.

Jones, A. and Oldfield, A. (1999) 'Sharing sessions with John.' In J. Hibben (ed) *Inside Music Therapy: Client Experiences.* Gilsum, NH: Barcelona Publishers.

Juslin, N. and Sloboda, J. (2001) *Music and Emotion, Theory and Research.* Oxford: Oxford University Press.

Kazdin, A. (1982) *Single Case Research Designs: Methods for Clinical and Applied Settings.* Oxford: Oxford University Press.

Kim, G. (1996) 'The shared experience of music therapy with the autistic child, viewed from a psychodynamic perspective.' MA thesis, Anglia Polytechnic University.

Lecourt, E. (1991) 'Off-beat music therapy: a psychoanalytic approach to autism.' In K. Bruscia (ed) *Case Studies in Music Therapy.* Philadelphia, PA: Barcelona Publishers.

Levinge, A. (1990) 'The use of I and me: music therapy with an autistic child.' *Journal of British Music Therapy 6,* 2, 325–339.

Mahlberg, M. (1973) 'Music therapy in the treatment of an autistic child.' *Journal of Music Therapy* *10*, 4, 189–193.

Magee, W. and Burland, K. (2006) 'Integrating electronic music technologies in music therapy practice: preliminary findings of a research study.' Paper presented at the annual music therapy conference, The Sound of Music Therapy, 2006. Proceedings published by the British Society for Music Therapy.

Mahns, B. (1988) 'Musictherapeutische Ansätze in der Praxis mit autistischen Kindern und Jugendlichen.' *Musiktherapeutische Umschau 9*, 68–78.

Mengedoht, T. (1988) 'Begegnung mit Karin.' *Musiktherapeutische Umschau 9*, 89–99.

Miller, S.B. and Toca, J.M. (1979) 'Adapted melodic intonation therapy: a case study of an experimental language program for an autistic child.' *Journal of Clinical Psychiatry 40*, 201–203.

Morley, S. and Adams, M. (1989) 'Some simple statistical tests for exploring single-case time-series data.' *British Journal of Clinical Psychology 28*, 1–18.

Morley, S. and Adams, M. (1991) 'Graphical analysis of single-case time series data.' *British Journal of Clinical Psychology 30*, 97–115.

Nelson, D.L., Anderson, V. and Gonzales, A. (1984) 'Music activities as therapy for children with autism and other pervasive developmental disorders.' *Journal of Music Therapy 21*, 100–106.

Newson, E. (2001) 'The pragmatics of language: remediating the central deficit for autistic 2–3 year olds.' In J. Richer and S. Coates (eds) *Autism: The Search for Coherence.* London: Jessica Kingsley Publishers.

Nordoff, P. and Robbins, C. (1971) *Therapy in Music for Handicapped Children.* London: Victor Gollancz.

Nordoff, P. and Robbins, C. (1977) *Creative Music Therapy.* New York: John Day Co.

Notomi, K. (2001) 'Behaviour management of children with autism: educational approach in Fukuoka University of Education, Japan.' In J. Richer and S. Coates (eds) *Autism: The Search for Coherence.* London: Jessica Kingsley Publishers.

Oldfield, A. (1993) 'A study of the way music therapists analyse their work.' *Journal of British Music Therapy 7*, 1, 14–22.

Oldfield, A. (1995) 'Communicating through music: the balance between following and initiating.' In T. Wigram, R. West and B. Saperston (eds) *The Art and Science of Music Therapy: A Handbook.* Chur, Switzerland: Harwood Academic Publishers.

Oldfield, A. (2001) 'Music therapy with young children with autism and their parents, developing communication through playful musical interactions specific to each child.' In D. Aldridge *et al.* (eds) *Music Therapy in Europe.* Rome: ISMEZ Publications.

Oldfield, A. (2004) 'Music therapy with children on the autistic spectrum, approaches derived from clinical practice and research.' PhD thesis, Anglia Polytechnic University.

Oldfield, A. (2006) *Interactive Music Therapy in Child and Family Psychiatry.* London: Jessica Kingsley Publishers.

Oldfield, A. and Adams, M. (1990) 'The effects of music therapy on a group of profoundly handicapped adults.' *Journal of Mental Deficiency Research 34*, 107–125.

Oldfield, A., Bunce, L. and Adams, M. (2003) 'An investigation into short-term music therapy with mothers and young children.' *British Journal of Music Therapy 17*, 1, 26–45.

Oldfield, A. and Cramp, R. (1992) 'Music therapy at the Child Development Centre, Cambridge.' Training video produced by Anglia Polytechnic University, available from the British Society for Music Therapy.

Oldfield, A. and Cramp, R. (1994) 'Timothy: music therapy with a little boy who has Asperger syndrome.' Training video produced by Anglia Polytechnic University, available from the British Society for Music Therapy.

Oldfield, A. and Feuerhahn, C. (1986) 'Using music in mental handicap. 3: Helping young children with handicaps and providing support for their parents.' *Mental Handicap 14*, 10–14.

Oldfield, A. and Nudds, J. (2002) 'Joshua and Barry: music therapy with a partially sighted little boy with cerebral palsy.' Training video produced by Anglia Polytechnic University, available from the British Society for Music Therapy.

Oldfield, A., Nudds, J. and Macdonald, R. (1999) 'Music therapy for children on the autistic spectrum.' Training video produced by Anglia Polytechnic University, available from the British Society for Music Therapy.

Pavlicevic, M. (1990) 'Dynamic interplay in clinical improvisation.' *British Journal of Music Therapy 4*, 2, 5–9.

Pavlicevic, M. (1995) 'Interpersonal processes in clinical improvisation: towards a subjectively objective systematic definition.' In T. Wigram, B. Saperston and R. West (eds) *The Art and Science of Music Therapy: A Handbook*. Chur, Switzerland: Harwood Academic Publishers.

Pavlicevic, M. (1997) *Music Therapy in Context: Music, Meaning and Relationship*. London: Jessica Kingsley Publishers.

Plahl, C. (2000) *Entwicklung fördern durch Musik: Evaluation Musiktherapeutischer Behandlung*. Münster, Germany: Waxman.

Prevener, W. (2000) 'Musical interaction and children with autism.' In S. Powell (ed) *Helping Children with Autism to Learn*. London: David Fulton Publishers.

Raffi and Whiteley, K. (1976) 'Willoughby Wallaby Woo.' Song on cassette tape entitled *Singable Songs for the Very Young*. Willowdale, Canada: Troubadour Records Ltd.

Reid, S., Alvarez, A. and Lee, A. (2001) 'The Tavistock autism workshop approach: assessment, treatment and research.' In J. Richer and S. Coates (eds) *Autism: The Search for Coherence*. London: Jessica Kingsley Publishers.

Richer, J. (2001) 'The insufficient integration of self and other in autism: evolutionary and developmental perspectives.' In J. Richer and S. Coates (eds) *Autism: The Search for Coherence*. London: Jessica Kingsley Publishers.

Robarts, J. (1996) 'Music therapy for children with autism.' In C. Trevarthen, K. Aitken, D. Papoudi and J. Robarts (eds) *Children with Autism: Diagnosis and Intervention to Meet their Needs*. London: Jessica Kingsley Publishers.

Ruyters, A. and Goh, M. (2002) 'Incorporating visual structure into music therapy for children with autistic spectrum disorder.' Poster presentation at the 10th World Congress of Music Therapy, Oxford, England.

Schmidt, B. (2004) 'Assistants in music therapy sessions.' MA thesis, Anglia Polytechnic University.

Schumacher, K. (1991) 'Musiktherapie mit autistischen Kindern als menschliche Begegnung.' *Der Kinderarzt 22*, 9, 1439–1443.

Schumacher, K. (1994) *Musiktherapie mit Autistischen Kindern, Bewegungs und Sprach Spiele zur Integration Gestörter Sinneswahrnehmung*. Stuttgart: Gustav Fisher Verlag.

Schumacher, K. and Calvet-Kruppa, C. (1999) 'Musiktherapie als Weg zum Spracherwerb: Evaluierung von Musiktherapie anhand des stimmlich-vorsprachlichen Ausdrucks eines autistisch-sprachgestörten Kindes.' *Musiktherapeutische Umschau 20*, 216–230.

Staum, M. (2002) 'Music therapy and language for the autistic child.' Available from: www.autism.org/music.html (accessed March 2002).

Stern, D. (1985) *The Interpersonal World of the Infant*. New York: Basic Books.

Stern, D. (1995) *The Motherhood Constellation: A Unified View of Parent–Infant Psychotherapy*. New York: Basic Books.

Stern, D. (1996) 'The temporal structure of interactions between parents and infants: the earliest music?' Unpublished paper presented at the 8th Congress of Music Therapy 'Sound and Psyche' in Hamburg, Germany.

Stevens, E. and Clark, F. (1969) 'Music therapy in the treatment of autistic children.' *Journal of Music Therapy 6*, 93–104.

Stewart, D. (1996) 'Chaos, noise and a wall of silence.' *British Journal of Music Therapy 10*, 2, 21–33.

Storey, J. (1998) 'Music therapy with children with autism and Asperger's syndrome within the context of a special school.' MA thesis, Anglia Polytechnic University.

Toigo, D.A. (1992) 'Autism: integrating a personal perspective in music therapy practice.' *Music Therapy Perspectives 10*, 13–20.

Toogood, R. (1980) 'Makaton vocabulary.' *Parents' Voice*, September, 1–3.

Trevarthen, C. (1979) 'Communication and cooperation in early infancy: a description of primary intersubjectivity.' In M. Bullowa (ed) *Before Speech: The Beginning of Interpersonal Communication.* Cambridge: Cambridge University Press.

Tyler, H. (1998) 'Behind the mask: an exploration of the true and false self as revealed in music therapy.' *British Journal of Music Therapy 12*, 2, 60–66.

Walker, M. and Armfield, A. (1982) 'What is the Makaton vocabulary?' *Special Education: Forward Trends 8*, 3, 1–2.

Warren, M. and Spinks, D. (1982) 'The Snake and the Goose.' Song on cassette tape entitled *Songs of Speech.* Leicester: Taskmaster Ltd.

Warwick, A. (1988) 'Questions and reflections on research.' *Journal of British Music Therapy 2*, 2, 5–8.

Warwick, A. (1995) 'Music therapy in the education service: research with autistic children.' In T. Wigram, B. Saperston and R. West (eds) *The Art and Science of Music Therapy: A Handbook.* Chur, Switzerland: Harwood Academic Publishers.

Warwick, A. (2001) 'I have a song – let me sing: relating part of a journey through music therapy with an autistic boy.' In J. Richer and S. Coates (eds) *Autism – The Search for Coherence.* London: Jessica Kingsley Publishers.

Weber, C. (1991) 'Musiktherapie als therapeutische möglichkeit beim autistischen Syndrom.' *Musik-, Tanz- und Kunsttherapie 2*, 66–74.

Wigram, T., Nygaard Pederson, I. and Ole Bonde, L. (2002) *A Comprehensive Guide to Music Therapy, Theory, Clinical Practice and Training.* London: Jessica Kingsley Publishers.

Winnicott, D. (1960) *Playing and Reality.* Harmondsworth: Pelican Publications.

Winnicott, D. (1972) *Holding and Interpretation.* New York: Grove Press.

Woodward, A. (1999) 'The emotional experience of an autistic child explored through music therapy.' MA thesis, Anglia Polytechnic University.

Yirmiya, N. and Sigman, M. (2001) 'Attachment in children with autism.' In J. Richer and C. Coates (eds) *Autism: The Search for Coherence.* London: Jessica Kingsley Publishers.

Zappella, M. (2001) 'Early intervention in autistic disorders.' In J. Richer and C. Coates (eds) *Autism: The Search for Coherence.* London: Jessica Kingsley Publishers.

Subject
Index

Note: The abbreviation SMPD is used for severe physical and mental difficulties

action songs 75, 146, 152, 208–9
activities of therapist, research results 183–4
Alvin model, free improvisation therapy 22
ASD see autistic spectrum disorder
Asperger's syndrome, Cynthia's case 136–8
assessment 45
    blank forms 196–7
    at CDC 42
    effect on child 123
    frustration of parents 125
    scales 160
    sessions 29, 46–7, 48, 51, 97
    units for group therapy 138–9
attention, ways of capturing 16, 22, 32, 34, 68–9, 110, 124
autistic spectrum disorder (ASD)
    case studies 45–61
    causes of 80–1
    control, need for 72–3
    increasing referrals 43–4
    music therapy literature 83–90
    musical interest 83
    treatment approaches 82–3
avoidance behaviours 80–1, 87

babbling, pre-verbal 19, 26, 59–60, 69, 99, 105, 111
balance, between following and initiating 68
behaviour difficulties, dealing with 25, 58–9, 72, 78, 133, 180–2

case studies
    children with ASD 45–6, 85–6
        Danny 51–2, 199–201
        John 47–51
        Joseph 46–7
        Leon 52–4, 202–4
        Peter 54–7
    children with no clear diagnosis
        David 119–24
        Lizzie 118–19
        Rose 124–5
    children with SMPD
        Jane 94–6
        Joshua 96–100
        Sean 100–6
CDC see Child Development Centre
chamber music playing, parallels with music therapy improvisation 33, 36–7
Checklist of Communicative Responses/Acts Score Sheet (CRASS) 160
Child Development Centre (CDC) 42–5
children
    individual needs of 126
    musical characteristics 30–1
    musical preferences 71
    with no clear diagnosis 118–28, 138–45, 191
    responsiveness of 106–7
    with SMPD 94–115
    with speech delay 118–19, 123
    see also case studies
clarinet
    aiding vocalisation 51, 96, 98
    allowing flexible interactions 47, 68, 74
    and dance/movement 53, 152–3
    in group therapy 144
    use of during therapy 24, 33–5, 183, 184
codes, video analysis 166–9
colour, musical element 31
communication
    active avoidance of 81
    balance in 68, 87–8
    children with SMPD 110
    child's unique pattern of 81, 82, 83, 126
    and 'contact' 87, 161
    early intervention 162–3
    evaluation of 88–9
    and group therapy 136, 146
    improved by improvised music 159–60
    improved by music therapy 52, 60, 160–1, 173–4
    music as non-verbal 18–19, 37, 38, 47, 66, 103
    non-verbal 18–90, 46, 85, 86, 88, 161
    parent–child 77–8, 158
    pre-verbal 19, 69–71, 74–5, 88
    scales 88, 160

communication *continued*
    with speech delayed children 118–19,
        124–5
    through attention-seeking behaviours
        72
    through movement 16, 74–5
    use of sign language 146
    see also vocalisations
concentration
    aided by group therapy 132
    improved by music therapy 54, 85,
        160–1
    therapist's 110
    ways of encouraging 148
confidence, building up
    of children 148
    of mothers 23–4
    of therapist 27–8
control
    ASD child's need for 50, 58, 72–3, 87
    behavioural approaches 25
    by therapist during group therapy 141
    children with SMPD 111–12, 153
    positive aspects of 72, 78
counter-transference 26, 110
CRASS *see* Checklist of Communicative
    Responses/Acts Score Sheet
Croft Unit for Child and Family Psychiatry
    42

Davies, Emma, research assistant 158–9,
    163–4, 168–9, 171–2
Dorian mode 33
dramatic games 71, 76, 112, 141
'dynamic form' 70

echolalic speech, reduction of 179–80
emotions
    advantages of expressing during
        therapy 181–2
    enhanced during music making 24
    expression of during therapy 86
    using music to express 96
    using the voice to express 111
engagement levels
    children 145, 168, 175, 178, 187
    parents 182

familiar songs/tunes 137
    encouraging vocalisation 67, 120,
        143–4
    linking sounds to movement 75
    providing structure 32, 48, 53, 101
    reassuring quality of 72

families
    discussions with 29, 45
    effect of having ASD child 56
    experience gained from 27–8
    gaining trust of 126
    group therapy 130–3, 146–7
    impact of ASD diagnosis 77
    joint working with 44
    in music therapy sessions 100
    observing music therapy 112–13
    see also mothers; parents
focused approaches 86–9
folk tunes 33
following and leading, alternation between
    68, 73, 87–8

games
    dramatic 75–6
    movement 142–3
    musical 49–50, 59, 71–2, 82–3, 88,
        121
    peek-a-boo 34, 57, 68, 202
    with ukelele 104–5
'Goodbye' activity 64–5
Grandin, Temple 84–5
greeting, in group therapy 140, 147, 151
group therapy
    children in pairs 136–8
    children in wheelchairs 150–4
    group rules 133–4
    membership 132–3
    multi-disciplinary 146–50
    musical material 135
    objectives 131–2
    preparations for 130–1
    review methods 134–5
    small classes 138–45
    see also music therapy; sessions

'Hello' song 64, 65, 195

imitation
    of child's vocalisations 48
    and learning to speak 69, 82
    of movements 74
improvisation 24–5, 32–3
    and avoidance behaviours 87
    clinical 69–70
    improving communication in ASD
        159–60
    and movement 143
    parallels to chamber music 36–7
    small group work 144

initiation of music-making 106–7
instruments
    distributing in group therapy 141
    playing bouts 175, 177–8
    as 'safe intermediary objects' 24
    single line 33–5
    therapist time spent playing 183–4
    vibrations from 83, 107, 151–2
    see also clarinet
'Intensive Interactive' approach 82
Interactive Music Therapy in Child and Family
    Psychiatry (Oldfield) 17, 19, 158, 192
'intermediary instrument/object' 24, 89
interviews with parents 171–2, 185

joint working
    with other professionals 44, 134,
        146–7
    with parents 44, 50

'Kamuthe', video analysis system 169

language difficulties 66, 127, 145, 146
leading and following, alternation between
    68, 73, 87–8
life experiences, therapist's 26–8
listening skills, encouraging 98–9, 124,
    147–8
literature reviews 83–90, 159–62

Makaton songs 146, 206–7
modal styles 33
mothers
    categories of 178–80
    confidence of 23–4
    guilt feelings 26
    involvement in therapy sessions 50,
        76–8
    mother–infant interactions 69–71, 82
    perceptions of children 160
    playfulness in 77
motivation 65–6, 110
movement 73–5
    analysis of 170
    in group therapy 142–3, 152–3
multi-disciplinary teams 37–8, 146–50
music therapy
    assessment forms 196–7
    focused approaches 86–9
    increased provision of 44
    interactive approaches 82–3
    literature 83–5, 159–62

previous case studies 85–6
referrals 38
specific approaches 89–90
stages 84
    at the CDC 42–5
training course 44
    see also group therapy; sessions
Music Therapy Charity 158, 188
Music Therapy for the Developmentally Disabled
    (Boxhill) 71
musical elements 30–1
musical games 59, 71, 88, 106, 121
'musical interaction therapy' 71, 88
musical interest, importance of 66
musical relationships, developed during
    therapy 25
musical structure 67

'negative' behaviours 78, 168–9, 180–2,
    187
non-verbal interactions 18, 26, 68–72,
    77, 124, 161
Nordoff and Robbins approach 84, 85,
    88, 161
nursery rhymes 33, 85, 122

parental involvement 76–80, 112–13,
    158, 160
Parenting Stress Index (PSI) 172, 185,
    186
parents
    advising therapist 112, 126
    aims of music therapy 23
    changes in behaviour 182
    discussions with 44, 113
    gaining trust of 126
    group therapy 130–1, 148
    guide to writing about sessions 205
    helping ASD children vocalise 71
    impressions of therapy 57–8, 185
    resentment 26
    role in therapy 45
    structured interviews 171–2, 185
    see also parental involvement
physical limitations 95, 107–8, 146
physiotherapists
    group therapy 146
    liaison with 108–9
Pied Piper (Bean and Oldfield) 135, 141,
    143
pitch 30
playfulness 18, 34, 75–6, 77, 119, 184

playing of instruments
    group therapy 141–2, 151–2
    research study results 175–8
positive approach 12, 18, 22–3, 72, 78–9,
    187
professionalism 38
PSI *see* Parenting Stress Index
psychodynamic approaches 86–7
psychodynamic theories 25–6
psychological models 25
pulse 31

referrals 38, 43–4
relaxation, music aiding 99, 109, 125,
    154
reports
    music therapy 199–204
    note-taking by therapist 44–5
    therapist research 173–5
research study 157–9
    aims 164–5
    hypotheses 162, 187–8
    interpretation of data 170–1
    methodology 162–4
    PSI results 186
    results 172–85
    structured interviews 171–2
    therapist reports 173–5
    video analysis 165–70
resistance, managing 25, 48, 49, 58, 73,
    121
reviewing, group therapy 134–5
rhythm, musical element 31

sessions
    assessment 29
    beginnings and endings 64–5
    parental accounts 106, 122–4
    room layout 63–4
    structure of 66–7
    therapist's activities 183–4
    video recordings of 17, 96–100, 102,
        113
    see also group therapy
sign languages 146
singing
    children with autism 89–90
    encouraging vocalisations 34
    see also songs
single-subject experimental designs 163
single line instruments, advantages of
    33–5

songs 206–9
    aiding communication 160
    'Hello' song 64–5, 195
    helping with naming objects 148
    importance of structure in 67
    see also familiar songs/tunes
speech
    children with delayed 94, 118–20,
        123
    development following music therapy
        48–9, 69, 99, 159
    echolalic 179–80
    speech therapists 37, 71, 88, 146
    see also vocalisations
stress levels of parents 172, 185, 186
structure of sessions, importance of
    predictability 66–7, 82–3

Tavistock Autism Workshop Approach 82,
    83
TEACCH programme 82
theme and variations 32, 144
'Theory of Mind' 80
therapists
    activities during therapy 183–4
    need for personal therapy 35
    outside musical interests 35–6
    relationship with patient 24–5
    role in multi-disciplinary team 37–8
Therapy in Music for Handicapped Children
    (Nordoff–Robbins) 84
timbre 31
training
    in music therapy 19, 35, 44
    videos 44, 50, 69, 96–100, 143, 144
treatment, ending of 39, 114
Treatment and Education of Autism Related
    Communication Handicapped
    CHildren (TEACCH) 82
turn-taking, improvement in 60, 99, 105

vibrations 83, 107, 151–2
video analysis
    forms 210–11
    in research study 158, 165–71,
        175–85
video recordings
    for research study 165
    of sessions 17, 102, 113
    training videos 44, 50, 69, 96–100,
        143, 144

vocalisations
    from basic exchanges 68–70
    children with severe mental and
        physical difficulties 111
    encouraged by music therapy 26, 49,
        50, 53–4
    research study results 179–80
    spontaneous 71
volume 31

'Willoughby Wallaby Woo' 143

Author Index

Aasgaard, T. 113
Abidin, R. 172
Adams, M. 163, 165, 169, 170
Agrotou, A. 70
Alvarez, A. 82
Alvin, J. 22, 24, 83, 84
Armfield, A. 146

Bailey, S. 73, 85, 86
Baron-Cohen, S. 80
Bean, J. 68, 135, 141, 143, 208
Benenzon, R.O. 89
Bergman, P. 83
Bettelheim, B. 80
Birkeback, M. 85
Boon, M. 100
Boxhill, E.H. 71, 88
Brown, S. 87
Bryan, A. 90
Bullowa, M. 74
Bunce, L. 165, 169
Bunt, L. 24
Burday, E.M. 159
Burford, B. 74, 170
Burland, K. 108

Caldwell, P. 83, 190
Calvet-Kruppa, C. 88
Carr, A. 25
Clark, C. 107
Clark, F. 159
Clarkson, G. 90
Coates, S. 23
Cramp, R. 69, 143

Darnley-Smith, R. 29
Di Franco, G. 88
Donna, C. 107

Edgerton, C. 159–60, 161
Escola, S. 83
Euper, J.A. 83
Evers, S. 159

Feuerhahn, C. 44, 146
Frith, U. 80

Gembris, H. 85
Goh, M. 89
Griessmeier, B. 113
Gustorff, D. 85

Heal-Hughes, M. 70
Holck, U. 161
Howat, R. 85
Howlin, P. 80

Janert, S. 72, 82, 83, 190
Jones, A. 49, 50, 51
Juslin, N. 24

Kazdin, A. 163
Kim, G. 86

Lecourt, E. 86, 87
Lee, A. 82
Levinge, A. 86

MacDonald, R. 44
Magee, W. 108
Mahlberg, M. 85
Mahns, B. 89
Mengedoht, T. 85
Miller, S.B. 90
Morley, S. 163, 170

Nelson, D.L. 86
Neugebauer, L. 85
Newson, E. 82
Nordoff, P. 84, 88, 180
Notomi, K. 82
Nudds, J. 44, 96
Nygaard Pederson, I. 21

Oldfield, A. 17, 44, 45, 46, 48, 49, 50, 51, 65, 68, 69, 96, 135, 141, 143, 144, 146, 158, 165, 169, 192, 208
Ole Bonde, L. 21

Patey, H. 29
Pavlicevic, M. 24, 69–70, 71
Plahl, C. 160–1, 169, 172
Prevener, W. 71, 88, 190

Raffi 143
Reid, S. 82
Richer, J. 80–1

Robarts, J. 70, 87
Robbins, C. 84, 88, 180
Ruyters, A. 89

Schmidt, B. 134
Schumacher, K. 87, 88
Sigman, M. 76
Sloboda, J. 24
Spinks, D. 207
Staum, M. 89–90
Stern, D. 26, 70
Stevens, E. 159
Stewart, D. 70
Storey, J. 82, 85, 86

Toca, J.M. 90
Toigo, D.A. 84
Toogood, R. 146
Trevarthen, C. 74
Tyler, H. 88

Walker, M. 146
Warren, M. 207
Warwick, A. 24, 80, 83, 84, 85, 86, 160,
    161
Weber, C. 84
Whiteley, K. 143
Wigram, T. 21, 22, 24
Winnicott, D. 24, 26, 88
Winter, U. 85
Woodward, A. 85

Yirmiya, N. 76

Zappella, M. 82